Translation and the Sustainable Development Goals

This book offers insight into the use of empirical diffusionist models for analysis of cross-cultural and cross-national communication, translation and adaptation of the United Nation's (UN) Sustainable Development Goals (SDGs).

The book looks at three social analytical instruments of particular utility for the cross-national study of the translation and diffusion of global sustainable development discourses in East Asia (China and Japan). It explains the underlying hypothesis that, in the transmission and adaptation of global SDGs in different national contexts, three large groups of social actors encompassing sources of information, mediating actors and socio-industrial end-users form, shape and contribute to the complex, latent networks of social engagement. It illuminates how the distribution within these networks largely determines the level and breadth of the diffusion of global SDGs and their associated environmentalist norms.

This book is an essential read for anyone interested in sustainable growth and development, as well as global environmental politics.

Meng Ji is Associate Professor at the School of Languages and Cultures at The University of Sydney.

Chris G. Pope is Assistant Professor at Kyoto Women's University, specializing in East Asian politics and communication.

Routledge Focus on Public Governance in Asia
Series editors:
Hong Liu, *Nanyang Technological University, Singapore*
Wenxuan Yu, *Nanyang Technological University, Singapore*

Focusing on new governance challenges, practices and experiences in and about a globalizing Asia, particularly East Asia and Southeast Asia, this focus series invites upcoming and established researchers all over the world to succinctly and comprehensively discuss important public administration and policy themes such as government administrative reform, public budgeting reform, government crisis management, public private partnership, science and technology policy, technology-enabled public service delivery, public health and aging, talent management, and anticorruption across Asian countries. The book series presents compact and concise content under 50,000 words long which have significant theoretical contributions to the governance theory with an Asian perspective and practical implications for administration and policy reform and innovation.

Translation and the Sustainable Development Goals
Cultural Contexts in China and Japan
Meng Ji and Chris G. Pope

For more information about this series, please visit www.routledge.com/
Routledge-Focus-on-Public-Governance-in-Asia/book-series/RFPGA

Translation and the Sustainable Development Goals

Cultural Contexts in China and Japan

Meng Ji and Chris G. Pope

Routledge
Taylor & Francis Group

LONDON AND NEW YORK

First published 2019
by Routledge
2 Park Square, Milton Park, Abingdon, Oxon OX14 4RN

and by Routledge
52 Vanderbilt Avenue, New York, NY 10017

Routledge is an imprint of the Taylor & Francis Group, an informa business

© 2019 Meng Ji and Chris G. Pope

The right of Meng Ji and Chris G. Pope to be identified as authors
of this work has been asserted by them in accordance with sections
77 and 78 of the Copyright, Designs and Patents Act 1988.

British Library Cataloguing-in-Publication Data
A catalogue record for this book is available from the British Library

Library of Congress Cataloging-in-Publication Data
Names: Ji, Meng, 1982– author. | Pope, Chris G.
Title: Translation and the sustainable development goals : cultural
contexts in China and Japan / by Meng Ji and Chris G. Pope.
Description: Abingdon, Oxon ; New York, NY : Routledge, 2019. |
Series: Routledge focus on public governance in Asia | Includes
bibliographical references and index.
Identifiers: LCCN 2018056814 | ISBN 9780367200725 (hardback)
| ISBN 9780429259470 (ebook)
Subjects: LCSH: Sustainable development–China. | Sustainable
development–Japan. | Sustainable development–Cross-cultural
studies. | Translating and interpreting–Social aspects. |
Communication in economic development.
Classification: LCC HC460.5.Z9 E555 2019 | DDC 338.951/07–dc23
LC record available at https://lccn.loc.gov/2018056814

ISBN: 978-0-367-20072-5 (hbk)
ISBN: 978-0-429-25947-0 (ebk)

Typeset in Times New Roman
by Wearset, Boldon, Tyne and Wear

Contents

Illustrations

Introduction

The United Nations (UN) Sustainable Development Goals (SDGs) offer a principled governance approach to supplement mainstream regulatory approaches that feature rule-making with an emphasis on compliance and enforcement (Young 2017). In *Governing through Goals* (Kanie and Biermann 2017), Steven Bernstein notices that

> even if the Sustainable Development Goals were perfectly designed … – fully coherent, built around consensual knowledge, action-oriented, with multilayered differential targets, and adapted to national capacities and circumstances – they would still require appropriate governance arrangements to diffuse them and integrate them into institutions, policies, and practices … the nature of the goals (SDGs) means that governance cannot rely solely on traditional tools of multilateralism.
>
> (Bernstein 2017: 213)

The key challenge of global governance through SDGs is to develop and implement new political instruments of social diffusion and sectoral mobilization to enable governments to 'promote the coordination and combination of policies to diffuse and integrate SDGs into global, country-level, and marketplace policies and practices' (Bernstein 2017: 214). Of course, the drive for SDGs stems from a multiplicity of global issues, injustices and inequalities. However, this book addresses the diffusion of SDGs in response to climate change and ecological destruction, focusing particularly on transitioning to new methods of energy production and consumption in China and Japan for reasons as shall be discussed. Global governance is simply one of a multitude of transformational responses to ecological destruction, which exert sizeable but not altogether predictable influences over changes in political and economic formulations whether on a global or national scale. Indeed, proactive strategies of climate change mitigation, ranging from buying fluorescent lightbulbs, shutting down greenhouse gas emitting factories, to geoengineering our climate systems, are still being developed and employed to mitigate weather extremities or pollution. However, a sizeable degree of reactive 'adaptation' is necessary given that the possibility of rapid and timely climate abatement has vanished, at the very least for the global poor (Thompson 2010; Mann and Wainwright 2018: 28). Putting to one side (for now), how the term operates as a metaphor of evolution to ascribe implicitly a sense of functionalism to social systems and social life, thus obfuscating its clear political and ideological content (see Mann and Wainwright 2018: 68–72), adaptation signifies a clear admission that climate change, at least to a degree, is unavoidable and that its impacts threaten global sustainability and expose inconsistencies in modernity (Beck 2015).

In confronting this ominous challenge, climate change technologies are considered to possess political qualities or otherwise lend themselves to certain political configurations. Taking, for example, solar radiation management (SRM), alongside the associated risks of globally orchestrated climate regulation, its architecture politicizes 'the mutual interlinking of the climates of sovereign nations in a radically new way', which could create 'new modes of technocratic internationalism', further enervate national sovereignty in practice and concept, and weaken democratic governance (Szerszynski *et al.* 2013; Asayama 2015). Political and sociological theory has played the vital role of fleshing out the potential extent of how our political economy and social lives may transmogrify based on the perilous consequences of Anthropogenic climate change on our social systems and political economy. Visualizations of political and economic change have been bifurcated between a Hegelian model driven primarily by a 'collaborative cosmopolitan socio-cultural force' and a Schmittian model constructed upon an anti-democratic 'securitized state of emergency', a politics of fear and 'intensified local-national-global conflicts' (Beck *et al.* 2013: 3/9). However, a more detailed analysis provided by Mann and Wainwright (2018: 29), offers a pair of dichotomies to map out a matrix of potential transformations in the current global political economic order based on whether or not capital continues to expand and whether or not a coherent planetary sovereign will emerge. While a discussion of the current political theory surrounding climate change is reserved for subsequent chapters, the point must be made here concerning the almost unfathomable scope of potentialities regarding the transformation of the current political economic order in the face of climate change. This distinction is imperative because it evokes a message that is increasingly internalized within social scientific disciplines; that is, the need to examine the nature of the change brought about by climate change and its seemingly amaranthine consequences on human and non-human life.

As implied, one need not speculate too much on the economic, humanitarian, political and social ramifications of climate change, such as conflict, diaspora, disease, famine, and so on, to understand that its impacts are all-encompassing and irreducible to a pigeon-holed definition such as 'an environmental problem'. On this point, Mann and Wainwright state poignantly that:

> [i]f good climate data and models were all that were needed to address climate change, we would have seen a political response in the 1980s. Our challenge is closer to a crisis of imagination and ideology; people do not change their conception of the world just because they are presented with new data.
>
> (Mann and Wainwright 2018: 7)

The task of responding to climate change, then, is multifaceted. However, a major challenge is the successful communication of its perils to effectuate a change in people's conceptions of the world. While this issue of contested discourses on climate change is addressed in Chapter 5, it must be noted that the arena of global governance is no exception to this as it seeks to diffuse – that is, effectively communicate and instil – a set of environmental norms by encouraging (that is, largely, without obligating) states to commit to a series of environmental pledges as stipulated in the SDGs and other agreements. However, global governance through goal setting requires the development of and experimentation with a new set of political intervention instruments and social mechanisms to enable the effective diffusion and local integration of adaptive SDGs in national contexts. Put simply, the task of diffusing environmental norms to the state and its citizens/subjects is therefore both a *political* and *communicative* phenomenon. As a result, this book will develop and explore **new political discourse analysis instruments to advance the study of the social dissemination and diffusion of the global SDGs and their adaptation in national contexts. It will examine political change but its focus primarily is on the communication of SDGs which have given rise to thriving sustainable living discourses in distinct socio-economic systems and national polities.** As stated, China and Japan are selected as the foci of the book. This is because, albeit to varying extents, they are both countries that have embarked upon ambitious and challenging nationwide projects to transition to a renewable and clean energy system which are driven by the social diffusion, adaptive integration and sectoral capitalization of the UN SDGs. Further, they are two proximately situated countries that compete for influence within one of the geopolitical regions likely to be most affected by climate change and both possess markedly a different political economic order. Therefore, it is hoped that in developing new discourse analysis instruments, a comparative analysis of communicative patterns in both countries will both demonstrate the versatility and pliability of these instruments as well as provide an informative analysis for researchers of East Asia as well as global governance. Further, the selection of these two countries as the geographical foci of the book is motivated by the increasing geopolitical tension in the region with one power, China, seemingly on the rise and the other, Japan, seemingly on the wane in terms of regional and global influence. Further, the consequences that climate change will exert on the race for natural resources and raw materials, will pressurize both states in numerous ways. With China frequently outbidding Japan for Russian energy supplies (Hook *et al.* 2012), is it possible that China's drive to 'go green' will be offset by Chinese businesses simply relocating to surrounding countries within China's Belt and Road Initiative (BRI)? Moreover, as a result, will Japan seek to diversify its energy dependencies or will the state attempt to specialize in, hypothetically speaking, new innovations in nuclear technology based on the assumption of international marketability to compete with Chinese dominance? Further, as the polar ice-caps continue to melt, how will the opening up of an Arctic trade route impact on the international relations of both countries? The aim of this book is not to answer these per se, but rather offer a model to analyse comparatively the communication of environmental norms based upon the SDGs in both countries such that it might constitute a useful and insightful methodology to examine the nature of political and economic change within and between both countries based on political communication, as the effects of climate change begin to take their toll on domestic and international politics.

From a methodological point of view, the robustness and effectiveness of the empirical analytical instruments can be tested by using them to compare the historically distinct polities of China and Japan. The new empirical analytical instruments to be developed will enable the comparison of the two countries in their ongoing search for new social economic growth models built upon the general purposes and requirements for the governance of SDGs, especially the set of SDGs directly and indirectly related to renewable energy production and consumption such as *Affordable and Clean Energy*; *Sustainable Cities and Communities*; *Responsible Consumption and Production*; and *Partnerships for the Goals*.

This book's aim is to develop and illustrate empirical diffusionist models to analyse cross-cultural and cross-national communication, translation and adaptation of the United Nation's (UN) Sustainable Development

Goals (SDGs). For this purpose, we *propose, develop and test three social analytical instruments of particular utility for the cross-national study of the translation and diffusion of global sustainable development discourses in East Asia (China and Japan).* Our study will test the underlying hypothesis that, in the transmission and adaptation of global SDGs in different national contexts, three large groups of social actors encompassing sources of information, mediating actors and socio-industrial end-users form, shape and contribute to the complex, latent networks of social engagement. It does so in order to illuminate how the distribution within these networks largely determines the level and breadth of the diffusion of global SDGs and their associated environmentalist norms, knowledge of which is essential for informing policy-making at national and international levels.

Within the proposed networks of social engagement distribution, we develop three empirical models to gauge, first, the influence from main sources of information on industrial end-users; second, the mediating effects of the media; and lastly, the multi-sectoral interaction among sources of information and the media. Using advanced statistical methods centred on structural equation modelling, which is a methodological innovation in the field, we have pioneered analytical instruments that can be used as social intervention tools in evidence- based policy-making to measure, monitor and intervene in the development of these three social phenomena. The model affords researchers and policymakers a means by which the cross-national and cross-sectoral communication of environmental norms may be analysed. In the case of the former, the model may be adapted and indeed used as a means to identify patterns of communication to be subject to further quantitative or qualitative analysis as per the researchers' aims. For the latter, the model may constitute a means by which the social diffusion of global SDGs in response to climate change and environmental pollution may be evaluated and understood. A UN-led framework of global governance based on climate change is, at present, one which attempts to identify ways in which the political economic order of the day may survive the challenges of climate change. As discussed in Chapter 5, this has entailed to a large extent relying on market mechanisms to facilitate the transition to renewable energies among member states, meaning that there is a pressing demand to identify and operationalize environmentally compatible models of economic growth.[1] Here, the new empirical analytical instruments developed will enable the comparison of the two countries in their ongoing search for new social growth models built upon the general purposes and requirements for governance of SDGs, especially the set of SDGs related to renewable energy production and consumption that lies at the core of the new sustainable living discourse in both countries.

This book draws on a wide range of literature in sociological research to build empirical diffusionist models to analyse cross-cultural and cross-national adaptation of the UN's SDGs. Our study argues that nations are embarking on a joint effort towards designing and implementing environmentally sustainable socio-economic infrastructures to respond to the epiphenomena of climate change such as water and food scarcity, fossil fuel dependency, extreme weather events, and so forth. For this purpose, we propose, develop and test empirical and novel social analytical instruments of particular utility for the cross-national study of the diffusion and adaptation of global sustainable development norms and values in East Asia.

Our study sets out to test the underlying hypothesis that, in the transmission and adaptation of global SDGs in different national contexts, three large groups of social actors encompassing sources of information, mediating actors and socio-industrial end-users form, shape and contribute to the complex, latent networks of social engagement. The model constructed to explore the dynamics of environmental communication is the first of its kind and illuminates how the distribution within these networks largely determines the level and breadth of the diffusion of global SDGs across communicative platforms and their associated environmentalist norms. The model offers a utility to policymakers and communications specialists as knowledge over the distribution within these networks is essential for informing, critiquing and understanding policy-making at national level and international levels, with nations striving to meet targets designed and propounded by frameworks of global governance such as the UN and its affiliates.

This methodological innovation is applicable to a wide variety of fields and is largely replicable and adaptable to a variety of communicative and politically informed analyses. Its contribution here is to the fields of communications studies and environmental governance by a) exploring how the world is turning to a wide range of market and non-market solutions to respond to climate change, particularly following the Paris Agreement in late 2015, and b) offering a model over the communication and dissemination of environmental norms from global governance institutions onto the national polity which measures the dynamics of diffusion and hence offers a means by which to evaluate national responses to global governance countermeasures to climate change whether by contextualization at the national level or comparison at the cross-national level.

This book conceptualizes and hypothesizes the diffusion, cultural adaptation and political capitalization of the UN SDGs in response to climate change at a cross-national, inter-sectoral level by developing data-driven empirical analytical models using advanced statistical methods. Diffusion is essential for the development of international and regional cooperation at governmental, business, industrial, research and legal levels. Therefore effective communication across multiple social and industrial levels and among various stakeholders is of paramount importance to effectuate such change. There is no better example of this than with climate change where tremendous and coordinated global efforts to respond from all stakeholders of society are imperative in order to meet the aims of the Paris Agreement and keep the average rise in global temperature below 2°C (preferably 1.5°C) of pre-Industrial levels by 2100. The SDGs provide a framework by which countries are expected to respond to social and environmental dislocations in our current global political economy.

While many claim that the world is turning towards environmentally sustainable models of growth and development (see Chapter 3), in order to meet the aims and follow the metrics of the SDGs developed by the UN, nation-states are responding differently to meet different domestic demands. Two cogent examples of this are China and Japan who are seeking alternative visions of environmental and energy security which co-exist with ambitions of greater regional and international prominence. Due to this, it is an essential task also to analyse how environmental norms are diffused within a national polity and the trajectories of development that this implies. Therefore, our empirical analytical models will address and provide innovative solutions to the following research questions which can be directly exploited for policy-making and social intervention purposes.

1. How are SDGs diffused and communicated vertically (both top-down and bottom-up approaches) within national contexts?
2. What characterizes the networks of social engagement between higher-level sources of information which underline the socio-cultural and national adaptation to new environmental standards to meet the requirements of the SDGs?
3. What is the intermediary role of media in the social transmission and national adaptation of the SDGs?
4. How is the media leveraged as a social intervention instrument to achieve the desired information transmission pathways for the diffusion, adaptation and implementation of SDGs?

While the UN has developed seventeen large SDGs, for the purpose of our book, which focuses on China and Japan, we will study the diffusion, communication and social adaptation of four large SDGs: 7 Affordable and Clean Energy; 12 Responsible Consumption and Production; 14 Life below Water; and 15 Life on Land that are particularly relevant for this region and, indeed, have provided the backdrop for the new regional competition, dynamics between the two countries amid the growing waves of the production and consumption of renewable energy, natural resource preservation and social development. The model constructed is novel and provides enormous utility to those seeking to understand the communication of environmentalism cross-sectorally.

The case studies of SDGs will demonstrate how flexible the model is as it can be used to demonstrative contrastive patterns cross-nationally but also within a country cross-sectorally. This is carried out through a path-analysis where the models may be adapted to explore the top-down communicative influence from higher sources of information but also bottom-up influences to new environmental norms and practices as intrastate sectors and stakeholders negotiate and adapt to the targets set by the UN and filtered through the state. In addition, the model can also gauge the role of the media both as an intermediary institution that sits between the higher sources of information to socio-cultural end-users, and as a main source of information itself. It therefore provides a novel and original means to examine the cross-national and multi-sectoral communication of environmental awareness, including responding to climate change.

This book will include multilingual glossaries of the Chinese and Japanese translations of UN SDGs. We will also develop SDG-specific multilingual terminologies extracted from a variety of Chinese and Japanese sources of information ranging from governmental and political to industrial, business and the media. This book will be for students and academics interested in the general debates of sustainable growth and development, as well as for audiences with a particular interest in the regional development in East Asia, and its implication for the global environmental politics. International relations scholars may be interested in the differences in models of environmental sustainability pioneered by both countries which are seeking to exploit this new regional competition, particularly with regards to renewable energy but also issues such as food security, as well as the theoretical underpinnings of the model proposed which focuses on the role of global governmental frameworks on the national context. Political scientists and communications specialists may be interested in the dynamics of communication cross-sectorally within a national polity and comparisons therein cross-nationally. Sociologists and environmental governance researchers may be interested in the model of diffusion proposed and tested, and its implications over the national and global response to climate change, its implications on the everyday, social and political administrative frameworks, and so on. Linguists, discourse analysts, social constructivist international relations researchers and communications specialists also may be interested in the data-driven methodology and model constructed to test the diffusion of environmental norms.

Researchers in area studies, particularly Chinese, Japanese and East Asian studies, may be interested in the different national responses to environmental challenges and the implications of both countries' response to climate change respectively on domestic society and political, economic and security architecture in the East Asia region. Finally, readers interested in the shape and trajectories of global development as well as those interested in climate change may find this book extremely informative in terms of the adaptation process from the global governance issuance of new frameworks of environmentally sustainable development to the adaptation and implementation, respectively, at the national level, as the world inevitably responds to the dangers and perils of climate change. The book requires understanding of exploratory statistics commonly used in the social sciences as it makes an original contribution to the social sciences by combining qualitative political analysis with quantitative linguistic methods. The primary audience is a professional one. However, it is written in a manner suitable for the interested layperson also, given the universal relevance of climate change to people across all industries and societies.

The book addresses the changes taking place in the following three chapters, before discussing the issue of 'translation' and introducing our model. In Chapter 2, we introduce social diffusion theory and relate it to the issue of climate change, with a focus on the architecture of global governance and the impact of climate change on national polities. Chapter 3 discusses the current and major developments in response to climate change, and Chapter 4 provides a concise overview of development in China and Japan and relates them to the theoretical approach of this study.

Note

1 This is to make the assumption that such a model is possible under Capitalism.

1 The growing sustainability discourse

In the wake of the Paris Agreement (*Accord de Paris*) of 2015, many have suggested optimistically that the world is on the cusp of a possibly radical transition from carbon-based energy to renewable energy. Indeed, 2015 was a historic milestone in the world's response to climate change. It provides an appropriate starting point to discuss the transition to renewable energies. For in this year most of the world's nations agreed to the terms spelled out in the Paris Agreement, which was adopted by consensus at the 21st Conference of the Parties of the United Nations Framework Convention on Climate Change (UNFCCC). Nation-states across the globe, including China and Japan, the geographical foci of this book, jointly were brought together for 'a common cause to undertake ambitious efforts to combat climate change and adapt to its effects, with enhanced support to assist developing countries to do so' (UNFCCC 2018). In the same year, the UN announced the Sustainable Development Goals (SDGs), abbreviated hereon as 'UN SDGs', which comprise a universal set of targets and indicators that 'UN member states will be expected to use to frame their agendas and political policies over the next 15 years' (Ford 19 January 2015). While this covers a range of issues and the UN makes no formal connection between the UN SDGs and the Paris Agreement, both set out an agenda to socialize nations by imputing environmental norms into models of development and growth. That is, the goals do not simply fixate on greenhouse gas emissions in the energy sector but also incorporate actions needed to be taken in agriculture, forestry, heavy industries, transport, and so on. These require nations to cooperate with respect to terrestrial, coastal and marine ecosystems (Leong 14 December 2015).

However, though there are indeed a number of the reasons for optimism regarding the transition to renewable energy, which have formed the basis of this book, this discussion is carried out in the subsequent chapters. Here, we start with a more concerned and phlegmatic explanation over the drawbacks and limitations to these existing frameworks of global governance to contextualize the issue at hand. To begin, despite exciting developments in renewable energies technology and implementation, few would argue that the global political economy is not still heavily wedded to greenhouse gas emitting energy resources. Moreover, the US, one of the largest emitters of greenhouse gases overall and per capita, has signalled its intent to pull out of the Paris Agreement which itself 'contains no mandatory provisions to report adaptation strategies or commitments' (Mann and Wainwright 2018: 75). Further, while one major goal established in the Paris Agreement is to limit the average rise in global temperature to below 2°C of pre-Industrial levels by 2100 (Xu and Ramanathan 2016), this target by no means guarantees the planet's safety. For example, a systematic screening which used the climate model ensemble that informs the Intergovernmental Panel on Climate Change (IPCC) showed that there is no 'safe' level of global warming, with evidence of thirty-seven forced regional abrupt changes that will arise as the planet warms, eighteen of which occur even if the Paris Agreement is successful (Drijfhout *et al.* 2015).

In addition to this, despite the uncertainty surrounding 'safe' limits of planetary warming, Kevin Anderson and Alice Larkin (née Bows), two prominent climate change researchers, note that the impacts associated with a 2°C rise in global temperature have been revised upwards, such that 2°C represents 'the threshold between dangerous and extremely dangerous climate change' (Anderson and Bows 2011: 20). Limiting the planet to a mere '*dangerous*' level of climate change appears to be what extent the UN, as the global governing authority over the issue, publicly considers to be attainable and that assessment may be overly optimistic. Due to the very fact that there is no safe limit, staying well below an increase in global temperatures of 2°C is a task of seminal importance. Additionally, how rapid and drastic changes may combine is an issue of enormous complexity and identifying the proximity of oncoming climate tipping points is beleaguered with uncertainty also (Lenton 2013). Meanwhile, the planet has already warmed by 1°C and it is projected to rise to 3–5°C unless there is a rapid and unprecedented response, which, on balance, does not appear to be forthcoming. Indeed, a recent statistically based probability forecast suggests there is a 5 per cent chance of the world keeping to 2°C and a 1 per cent chance of temperatures staying below 1.5°C, the preferred target of the Paris Agreement, by 2100. With these being the widely accepted thresholds of statistical significance in social scientific research, then, we might conclude, even if only for emphasis, that the aims of the Paris Agreement are practically unattainable.

Nonetheless, the setting of the two targets of 2°C and 1.5°C in average global temperature rise is to encourage coordination to avoid climate catastrophe. This is considered necessary given that energy monoliths have declared the existence of 2.8 teratonnes of carbon reserves and the industry as a whole invested US$674 billion on exploration and development of fossil fuels in 2011 alone (Mason 2015). Meanwhile, substantial deregulation has occurred within the national polities of the perceived world-leaders of the international community, as epitomized by the US under the Trump administration (2017–). For example, in June 2017 President Trump signalled the US's withdrawal from the Paris Agreement in the coming years, at the same time as he supported enormous natural gas and tar sands projects – a kind of 'dirty oil' – in Alberta, Canada. These projects are advocated not only by key figures in the current US Republican leadership, but also by the comparatively socially liberal figures of the previous administration such as Barack Obama, former President Bill Clinton and senior Democrat Hillary Clinton, as well as the prime minister of Canada, Justin Trudeau (Mason 2015; Austen and Krauss 25 January 2017).

This inconsistent and, some would argue, irresponsible approach to achieving carbon reduction for the latter and outright refusal to acknowledge reality in the case of the former[1] serves not only to directly decrease the likelihood of the world meeting its threshold on global temperature rise, but also sets a precedent for the rest of the world in committing to the substantial reform necessary. Indeed, it is widely acknowledged that the global energy sector is a central component of geopolitical thinking among policymakers around the world. For example, the expansion of new hydrocarbon industries promoted domestically by the Obama administration were considered to play the dual role of bolstering US energy security and bridging the transition of global energy from oil and coal to clean energies (Grieves 13 October 2016), despite the empirically backed assessment that the substantial use of all fossil fuels, including hydrocarbons, must be phased out within the coming years for there to be a chance of the world keeping to the targets set out by the Paris Agreement (e.g. Anderson and Broderick 2017). Further, it is possible that the creation of these new hydrocarbon industries within the US led Saudi Arabia to let the price of oil fall, impacting on oil-exporting countries such as Russia and Venezuela and in a time of oncoming climate disaster causing an over-supply of oil and gas (Mason 2015: 248; Klein 2017: 77). Either way, signals emanating from global markets and the corridors of global political power do not suggest the full-fledged commitment necessary in order to respond efficaciously to climate change.

In addition, Oil Change International, an organization campaigning to promote the transition to clean energy, warns us that, in order to adhere to the Paris Agreement, every new and undeveloped fossil fuel reserve must stay in the ground (Oil Change International 2016; Klein 2017: 72). In fact, leading climate scientists inform us that 886 gigatonnes of carbon must stay in the ground for there to be a one-in-five chance of keeping global warming below 2°C. That is, starting from the year 2000. As of 2015, no more than 470 gigatonnes of carbon dioxide can be emitted to keep to 2°C, as approximately half has already been consumed, while there essentially is no reasonable chance of adhering to the 1.5°C benchmark without 'overshooting' and relying on Carbon Capture and Storage technologies to lower global temperatures (Johnson 4 September 2012; Mason 2015; Mattauch 9 May 2016).

For these reasons, it is widely accepted that striving to adhere to these targets demands the mobilization of all sectors of society and the international community. The response to climate change has therefore constituted a variety of actors, ranging from international organizations, state, market and societal actors, who have tended to adopt a 'problem-solving' approach to the risks of climate change. The aim here has been to accept and make the 'prevailing social and power relationships and the institutions into which they are organised' run more smoothly by addressing the source of a particular problem (Cox 1981: 128–9 in Hook *et al.* 2017: 193). Of course, the extent to which this practice has been successful is debatable, but the point emphasized here is that it is carried out within the established framework for climate action. Those who take issue with the so-called 'problem-solving' approach mostly do so on the grounds that this does not go far enough to *solve the problem*, given that the system itself is the *source*. Instead, it is argued that what is required is a transformation of the global political-economic order as well. For example, many suggest that the elite top-down approach to climate mitigation and adaptation as embodied by the UN will prove insufficient, if it has not done so already, and that more radical state intervention, a committed and relentless political activism and other non-market mechanisms are necessary to challenge the economic order that has resulted in the oncoming chaos, by, to a large extent, granting similar privileges to the fossil fuel industries through enormous subsidization. These may be considered a 'critical-theory' approach to climate change (see Hook *et al.* 2017: 193–4), in which these so-called 'prevailing social and power relations' and institutions are not taken-for-granted but called into question by considering their origins (e.g. Klein 2013, 2017), or how they are changing or may change in the near future (e.g. Szerszynski *et al.* 2013; Mann and Wainwright 2018).

To put this to one side, however, even if a sufficiently broad, global and rapid transition to renewable energy and other sustainable practices through frameworks such as the UN SDGs, which encourage state intervention and are reliant on market mechanisms, were attainable, such a transition would impact significantly on human lifestyles, as indeed would an insufficient business-as-usual approach to ecological breakdown. Thus either way we can assume that the existing model of economic production and consumption and the political order upon which it is established will be faced with enormous pressures to adapt, whether to a response with the requisite size, intensity and rapidity necessary to keep to the Paris Agreement by 2100, or not. This will likely create new modes of economic, political and social organization. However, even though the result of this transition remains an 'unknown', it does not demand an extensive level of prescience to adduce that the scope of possible scenarios in responding to climate change is, at the very least, extreme. Therefore, academic inquiry into the nature of change is highly relevant to the gamut of disciplines in the social sciences, as stated in the introduction.

Further, as stated, our aim is to contribute to the literature a corpus-based analysis into the social diffusion and communication of sustainable development discourses as the world strives towards achieving the goals established in the Paris Agreement and UN SDGs. Indeed, such frameworks aim to normalize an ethic of environmentalism to instil a commitment among states toward climate mitigation and adaptation. However, although put forward as mutually complementary strategies to tackle climate change, the definition over the contents and ways of implementation of these two approaches are left to member-states, meaning that 'room remains for states to *reinterpret* these international efforts' (van der Does-Ishikawa and Hook 2017: 101, emphasis in original). Due to this, not just in-depth analyses of the mechanism of global governance to combat climate change but also how this norm of environmentalism is 'translated' by the nation-state in terms of specific policies, social and legislative changes and so on, are also of seminal importance to monitor and assess the ways in which the world is responding to climate change. Therefore, the analysis focuses on introducing a formalized and largely replicable approach to the formulation and analysis of hypothesized paths that underline the communication of the state's national adaptation and utilization of international goals to achieve sustainability. Moreover, the model constructed and implemented in this book is designed to examine how environmental discourses and the norms that underpin them are diffused (or not) across different communicative channels and networks at the national and international levels. At the same time, it may be adapted, modified and improved by researchers to examine the nature of political communication regarding perceptions of environmental ethics, duties and responsibilities, as polities attempt to adapt and reshape in response to the impacts of climate change. While the model is explained in more detail in subsequent chapters, we first turn to an introduction of social diffusion theory and its relation to global governance frameworks such as the UN SDGs, which comprise the theoretical approach.

Note

1 That is, President Trump, who has stated that climate change is a conspiracy created by 'China' for a geopolitical competitive advantage. It is likely that other members of the administration have known the reality of climate change for many years. For example, it was discovered following an investigation by InsideClimate News, that Exxon-Mobil had known about climate change since the late 1970s, having conducted its own empirical research, but nonetheless proceeded to invest heavily in think tanks to spread doubt about the advance of climate change (Banerjee *et al.* 16 September 2015). As Klein (2017: 67) states, the reality of climate change was known long before the current Secretary of State, Rex Tillerson, became the company's CEO.

2 Social diffusion of the sustainability discourse

As argued in the previous chapter, the strategic aim of the Paris Agreement and the SDGs is to regulate state and business conduct such that they become more sustainable. However, although the SDGs are organized and pioneered by the UN, a global framework of governance, it is to a large extent the responsibility of the state to regulate the conduct of private businesses and citizens of a country to correspond with UN frameworks of governance. Further, as stated, the Paris Agreement contains very little by way of obligating the state. Rather, the emphasis is on '*responsibilizing*' through methods of socialization by, for instance, tying the norm of environmentalism to notions of prestige, status and honour within the international community. This, indeed, has been argued to be the case for China, whose drive to 'go green', by financing green industries and dominating burgeoning renewables markets, is beneficial to the state's international image as it constitutes a value that may be used to legitimate Chinese regional and international leadership in a similar way to G7 nations heralding the norms of 'freedom' and 'democracy' on the international stage (LaForgia 2017; Pope 13 January 2018). Additionally, notions of prestige have influenced Japanese international relations also, particularly in the context of increasing state influence over international politics as its economic size shrinks relative to rising powers in the international system (Dobson 2017; Hatoyama 2017; Stockwin and Ampiah 2017).

State approaches to regulating the conduct of businesses, civil society and citizens have been the subject of considerable debate within the academic literature. For example, there are claims that, whether due to the rise of individualism as the pervading cultural component of postmodernity or the emergence of fluid 'networked' social structures transforming our economic system based upon revolutionary technological advancements, the result of globalization is that the state may wither away entirely (Giddens 1991; Beck and Beck-Gernsheim 2002; Castells 2009). Conversely, others claim that the state has indeed transformed but to the effect of strengthening its political power through a sophisticated process of delegating responsibility (but not altogether transferring it) and offsetting accountability onto epistemic specialist groups, the market, society or the individual (Burnham 2001; Stoker 2002; Hay 2007). For the latter at least, as Jonathan Joseph (2012: 131) states, the view is that this 'does not replace hierarchical state power, but supplements it and offers new, subtler techniques that regulate from a distance'. This governmental approach is to encourage certain kinds of conduct among social actors, often the individual but also businesses and those actors that ostensibly comprise civil society.[1]

This 'governing from a distance' is reflected in the analysis over the communication of risk and responsibility between the state, market and citizen in Japan. Van der Does-Ishikawa and Hook (2017), focusing on media discourses surrounding the transborder issue of atmospheric pollution in Japan, demonstrate how the state off-loads the associated risks and potential harms to subnational political bodies, the market and to citizens. Through this process, they argue, the locus of responsibility to implement adaptation strategies to certain risks domestically has been shifting from the state to these other stakeholders through a 'gradual, covert persuasion communicated through the media' (van der Does-Ishikawa and Hook 2017: 103).

For China, 'governance from a distance' may be observed in how media regulation has been forced to adapt to the technological and economic changes that would have brought about an extensive diversification of media sources which challenge political control of media content. While this may have been argued to be conducive to the 'fluidization' of social structures as noted above, Chinese state regulation has been largely successful in militating against the market liberalization of media content. However, this has been carried out through a variety of means and effectuated numerous changes in the media landscape. For example, we have witnessed the emergence of newspapers focused on economic markets, particularly in major cities such as Beijing, Guangdong and Shanghai, reflecting a partial diversification of content, as well as the widespread engagement in political propaganda and indoctrination chiefly carried out by businesses that are state-owned or companies that are managed by the state (Kudō 2015; Yu 2017). Further, online media content has been managed by placing restrictions on private companies, supporting stated-managed or owned online news companies and content and other policies that have meant that news sources are highly concentrated, particularly in major cities, towards state- managed content to an extent that exceeds that of democratic countries (Yu 2017). This reflects two relatively different sets and possibly extents of challenges faced by both states respectively in effectively communicating environmental norms to businesses and citizens.

For this reason, we argue that with the metrics and directives for setting out a global agenda established, the state, 'responsibilized' by multilateral frameworks geared towards effectuating a global response to a transborder issue such as climate change, is behoved to communicate the ideal of sustainable development to different stakeholders such as citizens and businesses. However, owing to the differences in terms of structure and control between the state and the media, there are differing domains and extents to which each state respectively is able to diffuse this message such that it entails a response not only from the state but from businesses and citizens alike. Indeed, this is not to suggest that media communication is the only means by which a state can enact responses to climate change conducive to the aims and aspirations of global governing bodies. However, media communication is a vital channel by which possibly unpopular legislative changes may be strategically legitimated or through which environmental norms and practices may be diffused in order to regulate conduct nationwide in ways that new legislations cannot (at first), such as 'responsibilizing' citizens towards new eating habits, working styles, precautionary responses to health risks and methods of energy consumption (Hook *et al.* 2017). Recognizing the differences of states' respective capability to communicate new adaptive behaviours, we argue that the norm of environmentalism espoused by the UN as per the SDGs, must be transmuted to fit within the social and politico-economic confines of a national polity for each nation to respond effectively to new requirements to combat climate change. Further, this process of transmutation must rely on effective communication in order to be effective. For this reason, the study proposes, develops and tests three social analytical instruments within two national polities, namely that of China and Japan, in order to analyse and compare the diffusion and transmutation of environmentalism cross-nationally. We claim that three large groups of social actors, i.e. various information sources, mediating actors that comprise the popular media and socio-industrial end-users, form, shape and contribute to complex latent networks of social engagement able to play a critical role in determining the level and breadth of diffusion of global SDGs and the environmental norms they seek to impute.

Within this proposed network, our model offers three analytical instruments. The first affords us the opportunity to gauge the influence from groups of information sources on socio-industrial end-users; the second allows us to examine the mediating role of the media as a social intervention instrument or, put another way, an intermediary institution that 'sits between the governors and the governed' (Wood and Flinders 2014: 159); while the third comprises a means by which the researcher can calculate the extent of Multi-Sectoral Interaction (MSI) among sources of information and the media, and relate this to quantitative metrics of environmental performance.

The corpus-based analysis aims to demonstrate how different information sources develop, shape and communicate social engagement over climate change responsibility and response among different industrial sectors in the national polities of China and Japan respectively. These two countries have been selected as both aim to transform their energy infrastructure towards one more analogous to the production and consumption of electricity from renewables in accordance with the global agenda of the UN, its members and affiliates. The analytical instruments developed may be used as tools of social intervention in evidence-based policy-making to facilitate, direct and enhance the social diffusion of global SDGs and environmental norms. To this end, our study first discusses the two inter-related themes of 'transition' and 'translation', which underpin the global push to overcome the international political economy's dependence on fossil fuels. This informs our theoretical approach where 'transitions' covers theories of social diffusion and relates them to current developments, changes and breakthroughs in responding to climate change, before focusing explicitly on shifts towards renewable energy in the two target countries.

Following this, we address 'translation', which underscores the role of social accountability, MSI and the media as an instrument of social intervention. Second, we elucidate the research methodology and the steps taken to implement structural equation modelling to discourses of sustainable development and transitioning towards a social and energy infrastructure based upon renewable energy and environmental norms in both China and Japan. Discussion then turns to the results of the corpus-based analysis including the attribution of social accountability, MSI, the role of the media as an instrument of social intervention and the important implications of our analysis for policymakers. Finally, our study concludes and considers the strengths and limitations of the model in discerning the role of individual actors and its implications over the characterization of social diffusion as both nations take action to avert the risk of climate change catastrophes.

It is a widely held view that in order to avert the consequences of extremely dangerous climate change, both policies of risk mitigation and adaptation of behaviours are necessary. Further, all sectors of society and the economy, not just policymakers, are required to respond at the earliest opportunity. As we shall see in the following subsection, a growing number of technological innovations and policy breakthroughs indicate a transition to renewable energies in time is possible, albeit unlikely. In order to effectuate change in people's everyday lives, business practices and indeed political priorities, multilateral institutions such as the UN have sought to diffuse the norm of environmentalism across a variety of social systems (on norm diffusion, see Jinna and Lindsay 2016; Joshi and O'Dell 2016). Efficacious and timely change might be expected to follow the diffusion of information from an authoritative institution such as the IPCC that functions to bridge the divide between the scientific and political communities (Asayama and Ishii 2012). Simply making the empirically backed case that, if societal and business practices do not change, then environmental degradation will imperil our civilization is not enough, though. For this reason, we review the literature on the sociological theory of diffusion and its relationship with the climate change dilemma.

Due to limitations of space, the review here is succinct, leaving comprehensive reviews of institutionalism and the sociological theory of diffusion to authors such as Strang and Meyer (1993), Schmidt (2008), Greenwood *et al.* (2008) and Wakuta (2016), among others. Here, we agree that diffusion refers to 'the socially mediated spread of some practice within a population' (Strang and Meyer 1993: 487). In an oft-cited quote, Rogers asserts that 'diffusion is the process by which an innovation [or practice] is communicated through certain channels over time among the members of a social system' (Rogers 2010: 35; see also Strang and Meyer 1993: 487–8; Wakuta 2016). According to Rogers, diffusion is a special type of communication: that is, it is concerned with spreading messages that are taken to be new ideas. There are four main elements in this process, as he outlines (2010: 35):

1.   An innovation, or practice (see Strang and Meyer 1993: 507).
2.   Certain channels through which it is communicated.
3.   A period of time necessary for its diffusion.
4.   A social system and its members.

Further, for institutionalization to take place, these innovations, practices and behaviours must first become taken-for-granted among the members of a social system. It thus requires legitimization for it to become, in time, a self-evident truth. While the literature is replete with discussion of how to define legitimization precisely and comprehensively, its conceptualization in sociological theory has developed largely from Weber's ideas regarding legitimacy, namely, it is a result of conformity with general social norms and formal laws (Weber 1978 in Deephouse and Suchman 2008: 50). Legitimacy is considered to be 'a generalized perception or assumption that the actions of an entity are desirable, proper or appropriate within a socially constructed system of norms, values, beliefs and definition' while 'taken-for-grantedness' relates to the extent to which a practice has become the object of habit and socially recognized as natural and plausible. In other words, both legitimacy and 'taken-for-grantedness' are necessary conditions for successful institutionalization (Suchman 1995: 574 in Wakuta 2016: 340; Wakuta 2016: 340–1).

In the case of responding to climate change, legitimating new and sustainable behaviours, whether in business practices or society in general, calls on us to explicate the validity and appropriateness of these new behaviours. Additionally, in order to increase the 'taken-for-grantedness' of new innovations and practices, it is necessary to incorporate them into the routine of an organization, whether through formal laws or sociocultural norms, and to effectively communicate these new innovations or practices to the members of the organization or social system (Wakuta 2016: 341). For self-evident reasons, then, effective communication and exposure to new messages is an integral component of institutionalization and social diffusion. Given today's plethora of information sources, an explanation as to why there must be a rapid and large-scale response to climate change satisfies the moral, material and pragmatic dimensions of legitimacy. However, the communication of climate change and the diffusion of new innovations to respond to it has been limited, as illustrated by the world's spending of an estimated US$554 billion on subsidizing the fossil fuel industry (Morales and Nicola 3 November 2014 in Mason 2015: 249). Further, in the case of the US, we see a heavily funded climate change counter-movement, though climate change denial is by no means limited to a single country. This comprises 'a large number of organizations, including conservative think tanks, advocacy groups, trade associations and conservative foundations, with strong links to sympathetic media outlets and conservative politicians' where a large portion of its funding is untraceable 'dark money' (Brulle 2013). As Brulle (2013) points out, this organized campaign of climate change denial constitutes an institutionalized effort to turn anthropogenic climate change into a controversy, whether for financial or ideological motivations or both (Oreskes and Conway 2010). On top of this, technological developments in the mass media have contributed to the emergence of the 'personally mediated society' (Bennett and Iyengar 2008: 723) in which climate change is seldom afforded the coverage one might reasonably expect an oncoming threat to civilization warrants. The lack of public exposure to this civilizational risk reduces the salience of an issue where the effects are either minimal or nascent, within the shared knowledge of an epistemic community (on epistemic community, see Haas 1992; Jagers and Stripple

2003). At least part, if not all, of the reason for these changes in the media arise from market pressures and, in some cases, political pressure, which in combination effectuate a 'nihilistic' media system less devoted to scrutiny of threatening and unpopular issues, and more focused on entertainment and viewership (West 2005).

Alongside this, we are witnessing an explosion of technology able to exert an increasingly sizeable impact on how individuals interact with the media system. Here, viewers are profiled and those profiles are then tailored to certain streams of revenue such as news stories or advertisements (and sometimes advertisements portrayed as news stories) where certain social networking companies are able to exploit users' web-browsing data based on computational algorithms which determine what news stories are made available to passive consumers. One of the results of this is that despite the problematic nature of pre-existing media communication, in the era of 'old media' a wide variety of individuals were exposed to the same information regardless of their political inclinations while with the rise of social networking platforms and commercial news networks, exposure to the news is becoming increasingly fragmented and selective. The result has been a decline in the number of those engaged on certain issues and, for those who are engaged, the polarization of opinion (Bennett and Iyengar 2008). Writing on the topic of politics, Bennett and Iyengar (2008: 723) state:

> [A] media environment featuring an abundance of consumer choice implies first that we will witness increasing inequality in the acquisition of political information. The 'haves' will find it easier to keep abreast of political events and the 'have-nots' will find it easier to ignore political discussion altogether. Second, the increased availability of information implies an important degree of selective exposure to political information. Among the relatively attentive stratum, partisans will gravitate to information from favored sources, while ignoring sources or arguments from the opposing side. Meanwhile, the large ranks of inadvertent citizens will continue to elude those who attempt to communicate with them, fueling the costs of political communication, while diminishing the effects.

Two points are germane. First, the words of Bennett and Iyengar resonate with the issue of climate change and the successful communication of strategies of mitigation and adaptation that require collective and coordinated engagement. Second, the diversity of sources online, in press and on the airwaves means that engaged consumers may indeed favour certain sources over others and thus remain ignorant of counter-arguments on certain issues as time passes. However, this may happen to passive consumers of the news on particular social networking websites also who are unaware that certain news stories are being selected over others and channelled to them based on their online profile in a positive feedback loop.

This results in three different types of consumers: those concerned about climate change are likely to receive news articles about its impact; those convinced it is a hoax are likely to receive articles to this effect; and those that chiefly engage with other issues or passively consume the news are much less likely to be exposed to the issue through these platforms. For all cases, those remaining unaware of this profiling of consumer to content may be forgiven for equating the news they receive as an unbiased and representative portrayal of global affairs. Moreover, while news sources are far more heterogeneous than in the 'old media era', particularly for the younger generation, the online platforms able to channel news information to match consumer profiles are, to an extent, homogenizing and have largely oligopolized.[2]

This can have the effect of polarizing the opinion of those that do 'consume' news on climate change while, perhaps more damagingly, those who believe in the existence of climate change are seldom exposed to news stories of its severity if their profile does not match the content – regardless of the importance of the issue. As a consequence, the processes by which members of a social system form socially shared convictions to respond to climate change are affected, despite many public opinion polls providing evidence that the majority of people believe in climate change and think action should be taken. Put simply, little discussion on climate change takes place and by the time that discussion grows in salience to the degree by which an effective response could be marshalled, it may already be too late (Marshall 2014). Furthermore, it is within this media landscape that environmental issues and debates are impacted by the 'struggle for visibility' (Thompson 2005). Of course, the emergence of networked digital communications technology and use has changed conditions for visibility over environmental issues, allowing activists to provide news and overcome barriers to journalism and the spread of information. However, commercial and public services are also able to negotiate a mediated visibility by investing heavily into public relations, image management and monitoring opponents, as well as focusing on secrecy and restricting the freedom of access to information (Lester and Hutchins 2012: 849). It is therefore an important task to subject what Lester and Hutchins (2012: 850/860) denote 'the strategic utility of invisibility' in a 'multimodal, multichannel and multiplatform environment' to academic scrutiny, despite the difficulties associated with analysing 'what is not there' as opposed to 'what is there'. Indeed, this problem is succinctly explained by Lester and Hutchins, as follows:

Generating evidence about the purposeful cloaking of political activity presents obvious methodological issues. It is one challenge to identify the issues and opinions that actively compete for attention but fail to appear on the public record, the sources that speak but are not quoted in published copy and press releases, or the facts that are presented to journalists that they subsequently disregard. These tasks, however, are distinct from the larger challenge of identifying the issues and events that are deliberately rendered invisible by sources and which are purposefully kept hidden for a period of time. More perplexing still is how to reveal why and under what conditions invisibility emerges as a desirable objective for activists and political groups, especially when they are trained and practiced at pursuing visibility in order to maximize their symbolic power.

(Lester and Hutchins 2012: 850)

While this model falls short of addressing some of the issues raised, as explained below, it does seek to provide a tentative measurement for the visibility-invisibility scale regarding certain environmental issues. Further, the model may be adapted to other research in order to understand the degrees to which certain actors in the communication of environmental issues are able to mediate their visibility at certain times. Before turning to a discussion of the research methodology, however, we first provide a concise overview of the considerable and timely technological and legislative breakthroughs that suggest the world may be on the cusp of transitioning to renewable energy, before discussing the relationship between social diffusion and effective communication in the subsequent chapters.

Notes

1 For a more in-depth analysis of this kind of governmental approach, see Hay (2007), Nadesan (2010), Joseph (2012), Fawcett *et al.* (2017).
2 Though, of course, the old media system had its setbacks in this regard, too.

3 Current developments towards renewable energy

A huge, global transition to renewable energies is underfoot, coming in a variety of forms. We have witnessed legislative changes among polities, particularly of the global south such as Bolivia, which has passed laws granting rights to nature (*Ley de Derechos de la Madre Tierra*), but also in other nations. We have also witnessed the emergence of new frameworks of development such as open-source technologies which focus on 'democratizing' as opposed to 'capitalizing' technology for quicker deployment and advancement. One example is the OpenAg Initiative, which, in the face of a global food crisis in tandem with climate change and enormous change in global population demographics, aims to construct open-sourced 'food computers', a controlled-environment agriculture platform which can mimic the specific conditions required to grow a desired crop and can be used to research and share data on plant phenology and growth (Ferrer *et al.* 2017). In addition, we see a rise of activism calling for a transition to renewables globally, particularly among indigenous populations (e.g. Indigenous Climate Action 2017; 350.org n.d.; People's Climate Movement n.d.) and a rise in small-scale, collaborative peer-to-peer initiatives such as co-ops and credit unions (Bibby 5 July 2013; Locavesting 7 November 2017). All this is occurring at a time when empirical studies demonstrate that switching to 100 per cent renewable and clean energy (i.e. wind, water and solar) is eminently achievable, and necessary, for most of the world's nations before 2050, including China and Japan (Jacobson 2017).

Further, there is an economic incentive for consumers and private enterprises alike as potentially epoch-breaking changes in technological development and market conditions have seen many states and businesses commit themselves to a complete and rapid transition to renewable energy, albeit within the context of enormous state intervention. For example, China has signalled its intent to close down over 1000 coal burning plants (*Reuters* 22 February 2016), while numerous news outlets make sensationalist claims, though not unfounded, such as those made by the chairman of

Ford in the *New York Times*, claiming that China will lead the electric car future (Bradsher 5 December 2017) or others; for example, that China is winning the electric cars 'arms race' (Shane 20 November 2017).

Geopolitical or mercantilist considerations aside, transitioning to renewable energy has created jobs across the board, contributing to the economy of countries worldwide. For example, development in wind energy has already created millions of jobs in China, Japan and other countries including the US, and the rate of job growth is accelerating (see Hamilton and Liming September 2010; Jacobson 2017). Further, a host of nations including the enormous and growing Asian economies of China and India have committed themselves to transitioning the nation's infrastructure towards electric vehicles as one means to offset their carbon emissions in the near future (Wattles 3 June 2017; Morris 10 September 2017; Bradsher 5 December 2017). Meanwhile, in Latin America, Chile has negotiated a contract which will result in the cheapest unsubsidized electricity ever produced, half the price of coal (Dezem 19 August 2016; Lombrana 31 March 2017), while in the Middle East Abu Dhabi and Dubai are pursuing similar projects which vastly outcompete fossil fuels and nuclear power (Graves 1 March 2017, 5 June 2017). On top of these developments, major automobile manufacturers are switching *en masse* to electric and hybrid models (e.g. Vaughn 5 July 2017; Estrada 28 September 2017; Coren 22 October 2017), while new chemistries are causing new and transformatory batteries to enter the market (Chandler 22 March 2016; Hall 8 March 2017; Morris 9 April 2017) and developments in biotechnology offer potentials for the mass production of low carbon oil substitutes (Stacey 16 May 2016).

Of course, development is not limited to the energy sector but extends across a broad range of industries including agriculture, healthcare, transportation and so on. To take one example, with the Living Planet Index predicting the Earth will lose two-thirds of vertebrate populations by 2020 compared to populations in 1970 (WWF 2016: 14), developments in genetics, such as CRISPR- Cas9, a cutting-edge tool in genome editing, could theoretically (without considering any ethical implications) help scientists to bioengineer ecosystems better able to survive under volatile climates (Bourke 12 September 2017). Another example of this is the development in materials science and nanotechnology which offers opportunities to overcome the issue of environmental pollution (Khullar 4 September 2017), including greenhouse gases, and to identify 'technically and economically viable solutions to the rapid deployment of renewables technologies' (Gielen *et al.* 2016: 119–20). Notably, these technological advancements are not solely explained by a poor level of efficiency in existing technologies.

For example, it is claimed that building wind farms in the right locations of North Dakota, Kansas and Texas would power everything in the United States already but what is lacking, aside from perhaps the requisite political courage or means, is large-scale investment in power lines to transport electricity across the US (Statoil 21 January 2015). On top of this, developing nations, under the right conditions, are able to leapfrog the development patterns of advanced nations, forgoing their 'Dickensian period' of rapid and essentialized industrial growth and its environmental and social consequences, to convert their energy and utility sector to renewables, with, for example, the emergence on the market of cheap solar panels which do not require connection to the main energy grid – simultaneously offering the potential to connect the global poor to the worldwide web (*The Economist* 9 November 2017).

These separate responses reflect different approaches to the same inevitable dual outcomes: first, a major change in the energy economy; and second, new forms of social organization upon which it is conceptualized and implemented. Legislative changes such as those carried out in Bolivia in 2010 reflect a potential transition towards a different social relationship with nature and energy informed by indigenous cultures, a view analysed and advocated by a number of environmental scientists (e.g. Boelens 2013; Linton and Budds 2014). In the face of the heavy, non-market subsidies granted to fossil fuel polluters, some doubt that the technological breakthroughs in renewable energies will have the scope, speed and scale of market mechanisms needed to respond in time to the climate change crisis, necessitating a change in the relationship between the producers and consumers of energy as well as other natural resources, for example food and water. State intervention in green energy development, which in the case of China partly reflects the state's fear of popular upheavals owing to the considerable health risks associated with domestic urban living, at the same time is indicative of a geopolitical and global economic ambition to become a forerunner in the global energy politics in the very near future.

This can be seen, for example, in the Obama administration's decision to impose tariffs on Chinese solar panels in 2012 (Mufson 17 May 2012). Finally, the rise of global governance frameworks, such as the SDGs and the Paris Agreement, have operationalized new metrics in environmental governance to evaluate and rank the actions undertaken by every nation in the world, which signifies the growing influence of global governance in disseminating new environmental norms and socializing states to direct their conduct towards a commonly shared goal. At present, whether a suitable response to climate change will prove possible is unknown; as is the kind of political system to be inherited from this transition should it occur. It is, therefore, worth considering the similarities and differences in the transition towards new systems of energy and environmental governance that are conducive to renewable energies. This is the task of the following subsection on China and Japan, two very different national polities seeking and competing for regional influence over the political and economic architecture of East Asia.

4 Development of clean energy in China and Japan

This chapter examines the transition to renewable energies being made by China and Japan, starting with the latter as the 'world's largest importer of liquefied natural gas (LNG), second largest importer of coal, and the third largest importer of oil and oil products' (DeWit 2015). Japan is the largest importer of LNG by a considerable margin, importing over double that of South Korea, the second largest importer, and over three times that of China, the third largest importer (International Gas Union 2017: 11). Meanwhile, China is the largest importer of coal, the second largest importer of crude oil albeit importing less than half of the number one, the US, as well as the third largest importer of LNG, as mentioned (Index Mundi 2017a, 2017b; International Gas Union 2017: 11). With concern for the environment growing, a number of new frameworks and metrics have emerged to measure and rank each country's commitment to environmental protection, including responding to climate change. One example is the Environmental Performance Index (EPI), developed by the Yale Centre for Environmental Law and Policy and the Yale Data-Driven Environmental Solutions Group at Yale University and the Center for International Earth Science Information Network at Columbia University in collaboration with the Samuel Family Foundation, McCall Macbain Foundation and the World Economic Forum (Hsu *et al.* 2016).

In 2016, the EPI issued a report detailing the level of environmental performance of individual states' policies, employing satellite technologies and remote sensing to ensure globally comparable data sets where 'national governments fail to monitor or report environmental data' (Hsu *et al.* 2016: 16). These metrics are not solely related to environmental protection but also to decarbonizing economic growth as markets respond to the economic and environmental benefits of green technologies. According to the 2016 report, Japan is ranked 39th and China 109th in the world in terms of each state's calculated EPI (Hsu *et al.* 2016: 19). Indeed, few would argue over the low standard of environmental health in China compared to Japan that the rankings suggest. For Chinese leaders have long prioritized economic growth at the expense of the environment, with claims of an attitude of 'pollute first, clean up later' prevailing throughout most of the twentieth century (Hook *et al.* 2017). Illustrative is the case of atmospheric pollution: approximately 99 per cent of the Chinese population lives in areas where PM2.5, a harmful particulate matter, exceeds the World Health Organization's (WHO) guidelines. Other issues, such as water pollution, in which up to 40 per cent of China's freshwater is considered a public health risk, highlight the threat to environmental health (Hook *et al.* 2017: 25–7).

At the same time, China's economic modernization has led to a rapid increase in the emission of greenhouse gases – as a huge exporter of material goods to dependent nations across the globe, including Japan – such that the country is now branded as the largest emitter of climate change pollution (Friedman 20 August 2015). However, while an important tool to spread awareness and reach agreements over the locus of responsibility in responding to climate change, the EPI index does not paint the whole picture. For instance, as with other industrialized nations, Japan is no exception to the environmentally damaging pattern of development either. A similar account might be made in terms of environmental risk for Japan's re-industrialization and modernization after the Asia-Pacific War. Here we see how the pursuit of social justice by those who bore the brunt of the cost of sacrificing environmental safety for rapid economic development was an arduous and gradual process that not all of those affected acquired (Hook *et al.* 2017: 32–7). Additionally, the exact scale of climate change pollution remains contested.

A report by Liu *et al.* (2015: 335), for instance, uses empirically backed data to analyse China's energy consumption. It shows that, although total energy consumption was 10 per cent higher in 2000–2012 than that reported by China's national statistics, the emission factors for coal are much lower than the default values recommended by the IPCC. These figures mean that China emits 2.9 gigatonnes of carbon less than previous estimates suggest (see also Friedman 20 August 2015). Moreover, despite China's low EPI score, owing partly to air pollution, recent modelling of China's contribution to global radiative forcing[1] has found the impact of pollutants is not one-way. For instance, pollutants such as sulphate particles, part of PM2.5, scatter light in a way to counteract some of the increase in radiative forcing (Li *et al.* 2016; Spracklen 2016). This suggests that tackling the issue of immediate health risks due to the inhalation of harmful particulates without simultaneously curbing greenhouse gas emissions may run the risk of greatly exacerbating the greenhouse effect. Furthermore, research on both China and Japan has led to claims that both countries respectively are rapidly responding to climate change and may even become world leaders in renewable technologies. Some of the main developments underway at present are summarized below.

China's position on responding to climate change was made clear by Xi Jinping, General Secretary of the Communist Party of China (CCP), in a speech delivered at the 19th National Congress in late 2017. The speech, which lasted over three hours, offered a vision of China's drive towards a new era, giving a comprehensive outline of the range of areas deemed necessary to reform or otherwise improve in order to realize the 'Chinese dream' (*Zhongguo meng*) of modernization. Aside from other themes such as clamping down on political corruption, strengthening the military, political reform and economic liberalization measures, environmental conservation and green development were prominently discussed. While modernization was seen to have been accompanied with enormous cost to the environment, President Xi sought to conflate the goal of modernization with environmentalism, stating:

> The modernization we want to establish is one in which man and nature harmoniously co-exist. We must create more material and spiritual wealth in order to meet the people's growing needs for a better life and also to provide more quality ecological products to satisfy the growing need for a beautiful ecological environment.
>
> (*Xinhua* 27 October 2017, our translation)

Thus, while the previous trajectory of the state's modernization had been deleterious to the country's ecological condition, the current stage of development in China demands a more eco-friendly form of growth for the nation to modernize. It must be stated, however, that the idea of a harmonious society where man co-exists with nature was advocated by Hu Jintao during his premiership, too (Zhang 2017: 490). Moreover, this does not necessarily imply a shift from the notion of shaping nature to one's will that characterized earlier stages of China's rapid development (Shapiro 2001; Hook *et al.* 2017: 25), given the employment of geo-engineering technologies to modify weather conditions in China such as cloud-seeding rockets in drought-prone and some highly polluted areas (Edney and Symons 2014: 320). Nonetheless, environmental conservation and protection do comprise a state effort to 'build a beautiful China' (*jianshe meili Zhongguo*), and to do so, developing and fostering an 'ecological civilization' (*shengtai wenming*) is considered necessary. Alongside this, President Xi also indicates that the role in responding effectively to environmental risk is government-led but also relies heavily on business actors as well as citizens: 'We will construct a government-led environmental governance system in which businesses constitute a main component and social organizations and the public also participate' (*Xinhua* 27 October 2017, our translation).

While cynics may claim the consequence of this 'ecological civilization' is that China's pollution and unsustainable resource practices are relocated to other partners of the 'One Belt, One Road' (*yidai yilu*) initiative, elsewhere called the Belt and Road Initiative (BRI), in a way similar to how Japan exported its own polluting industries in an earlier era, an infrastructure development strategy aimed at integrating Eurasian and other countries with China (Tracy *et al.* 2017: 77–8), China is currently undergoing a 'green shift' (*lüse zhuanxing*) in which industries are being compelled, and infrastructures developed, to pollute less. Further, President Xi has officially recommended that the BRI be implemented together with the UN 2030 sustainable development agenda (Ministry of Infrastructure and Information Technology, China 16 May 2017).

What is more, in 2016 China became the world's largest producer and consumer of renewable energy and the world's largest investor, contributing to more than 40 per cent of global increases in renewables output (Buckley and Nicholas 2017; *Xinhua News Agency* 23 July 2017). China now owns five of the world's six largest solar-module manufacturing firms, five of the top-ten largest wind turbine manufacturers and is world-leading in the global lithium sector, with lithium ion used in electric vehicles. Finally, between 2015 and 2021, China is expected to install 36 per cent of all global hydroelectricity generation capacity, 40 per cent of all global wind energy and 36 per cent of all solar generation capacity (Buckley and Nicholas 2017: 2; Slezak 6 January 2017).

This 'green shift' has benefitted from the passage of an increasing number of legislative instruments and actions supportive of the green agenda, resulting by now in the evolution of the country's environmental protection framework. For example, the 2005 Renewable Energy Law laid the groundwork for increased centralized action by the government to accelerate the transition to renewable energies by establishing a unified energy department, the National Energy Administration. New policy instruments include providing a framework for renewable energy development, electricity market inclusion of renewables, a feed-in tariff, which is a policy mechanism to encourage investment in renewables, renewable subsidies, favourable loans, as well as tax cuts and exemptions, and more.

The law was then amended four years later to further strengthen central planning and regulation of China's energy grid as well as to oblige power grid companies to allow renewable energy enterprises with the relevant governmental licence to access the grid and to purchase the full amount of electricity generated (Zhang 2017: 491–4). Alongside the global spread of renewable technologies emanating from China, we can also see significant domestic changes to China's energy system. For instance, China's Ministry of Industry and Information Technology (MIIT) asserts that the first official list of 'green manufacturing systems' to develop a 'green and low-carbon cycle' was released in 2017. It included 193 'green products', 201 'green factories', twenty-four 'green parks' and fifteen enterprises able to demonstrate the feasibility of 'green supply chain management'. The ministry further states that, in 2016, the output value of the energy-saving and environmental protection industry in China reached CNY5.1 trillion (at the time of writing, approximately US$771.6 billion), with China's production and sale of 'new energy vehicles' (*xin nengyuan qiche*) also the world's highest, and China's photovoltaic industry accounting for more than 50 per cent of the world's total output (MIIT 14 November 2017).

A sizeable shift towards renewables is observable in Japan, too. Abe Shinzō, prime minister of Japan, spelled out Japan's response to climate change at the 193rd session of the National Diet, the nation's bicameral legislature, on 20 January 2017, when he announced his administration's aim to increase the number of fuel cell vehicles (FCVs) from the approximately 40,000 vehicles in operation today to forty times as many by 2020. Further, he stated that Japan would build an international hydrogen supply chain, including not only production but also transportation and consumption, using the world's first liquid hydrogen carrier as transport (Abe 20 January 2017). This is part of building a 'hydrogen society' (*suiso shakai*), as championed by the Abe administration, which the prime minister states will function based on renewable energies (Abe 20 January 2017).

Indeed, while the official projection for the expansion of renewable energies in Japan's power mix by 2030 reaches only 22–24 per cent, according to the Ministry of Economy, Trade and Industry (METI), a comparable figure to China's power mix projection, this may simply reflect the lobbying of vested interests in the energy and utilities sector as other projections point to a far greater expansion in use given the potential and scope of public and private investment into renewable energy (DeWit 2015). For context, this drive for renewable energies may be seen as resulting from the Great Tōhoku Earthquake and Fukushima Daiichi nuclear disaster, referred to as 3.11 with it having occurred on 11 March 2011, in which approximately 20,000 people were killed, 390,000 people were displaced and the largest nuclear meltdown in mankind's history took place, the effects of which are not fully known (Ikeda 2013: 15; Nagasaka 2013: 7; Sekizawa 2013; Williamson 2014).

As part of the reconstruction process of the areas affected, verification projects are being carried out in Fukushima prefecture to test the feasibility of Japan transitioning to a completely carbon-free energy system from 2040 (Abe 20 January 2017; New Energy and Industrial Technology

Development Organization 1 August 2017). While the hydrogen society may in fact come to depend on Australian low-grade carbon, given the lack of hydrogen gas in Japan (Hanley 18 September 2015), the drive to develop, diversify and diffuse cutting-edge renewable technologies is considerable. According to Japan's New Energy and Industrial Techno-logy Development Organization (NEDO), the Fukushima model attempts to test the feasibility of generating electricity from renewable energy and then using that to power the conversion of water into hydrogen gas by means of alkaline water electrolysis, for the gas then to be transported nationwide and managed in a way to meet energy demand (NEDO 1 August 2017).

Central to the transition to renewable energies has been the rollout of the smart grid whose sophisticated technologies affords a more decentralized framework compatible with renewable energy from small-scale, local pro-ducers (such as households with installed solar panels) to large-scale produc-ers (such as wind farms). Though the smart grid and its associated appliances, such as the smart meter, have raised a number of important issues, such as privacy and data protection, given the large amount of personal data trans-mitted in real-time from consumers to providers (Yuasa 2012), the transition to renewable infrastructure is being carried out through enormous public and private funding. This has a dual function: it aims not only to respond to the effects of climate change but to revitalize local economies, too.

The strategy has been supported by a raft of new legislation designed to foster market competition in alternative energies. This includes the liberal-ization of Japan's electricity and city gas industries to give greater market penetration to renewable energies (*Japan Times* 7 March 2015), taxes on carbon to encourage investment in alternative energy (DeWit 2015), the institutionalization of the top-runner method, in which businesses must conform to the highest standard set across the entire industrial sector within a given time frame, to new sectors in order to force businesses to lessen their carbon footprint (*Kankyō Bijinesu Onrain* 2012), among others (DeWit 2017; Hook *et al.* 2017: 158–62; Johnston 14 October 2017). As a result, renewable technologies have spread in Japan up to a point where 46 per cent of the country's electricity needs were supplied by renewable sources for a whole day as measured on 4 May 2016. Further, over the course of the month, more than 20 per cent of the country's energy supply was found to come from renewables such as solar, wind, geothermal, hydro and biomass (Johnston 14 October 2017). Despite the conservative projections for the 2030 power mix, then, Japan's renewable energy sector seems able to achieve much more.

Both China and Japan have invested heavily in the smart grid and using smart technology to upgrade social infrastructures (DeWit 2015, 2016,

2017; Hook *et al.* 2017). China, for instance, places 'smart restructuring' (*zhineng zhuanxing*) and green development as core components of its China Manufacturing 2025 (*2025 Zhongguo zhizao*) initiative which claims to respond to the challenges of a new industrial revolution (MIIT 19 May 2015). While 'smart restructuring' in China and Japan expand into other sectors of the national economy as well as energy per se (Hook *et al.* 2017), its very scope has the capacity to vastly reduce energy consumption and the emission levels of harmful pollutants such as greenhouse gases.

In the case of China, the National Energy Administration issued a new action plan to accelerate the construction of distribution networks, where investment in the period from 2015 to 2020 is projected to amount to approximately CNY2 trillion (at the time of writing approximately US$302.6 billion), while already constituting 30 per cent of the world's total investment on smart grid technology (Mathews and Tan 2014; *Xinhua News Agency* 7 September 2015). At the same time, Japan has announced an economic revitalization strategy aimed at upgrading vast portions of the nation's social infrastructures with the use of information technology, in which renewable energy and energy efficiency play a central role contributing to both environmental sustainability and also a new model of economic development (DeWit 2015; Hook *et al.* 2017). Further, developments in renewable energy systems are not necessarily limited by national borders given proposal of an Asian Super Grid (ASA). The initial aim of the ASA is to integrate the energy supply and demand of most countries of East Asia and may even expand to Central and South East Asia. If carried out, this would lessen a state's dependency on fossil fuel imports and decrease regional tension concerning the transport of fossil fuel supplies (Mathews 2016). From this, we may conclude that there is ample evidence to suggest China and Japan are in the accelerating process of transitioning to renewable energies. How this will be carried out and its impacts on the social systems in both countries is another issue, however, as the next section seeks to show.

Note

1 Radiative forcing is a metric used to quantify the change in atmospheric energy due to greenhouse gas emissions (Carbon Offset Research & Education 2011).

5   Translation of sustainability

In our study, the word 'translation' is not confined to the translation of one language to others, but rather is used as well both in a general and figurative sense as a term to understand how the socio-political and economic changes resulting from the directives issued by competent international authorities within the architecture of global governance move down from the level of the nation-state to the level of the everyday lives of the citizens. It is hypothesized in our study that the social diffusion and national adaptation of SDGs requires important innovation in both the language and the knowledge translation of sustainability principles and social values. This is proposed as the dual mechanism of sustainability translation.

The issue of transition is broad in scope, giving rise to academic inquiry among political theorists and political scientists into the nature of change on the national polity, while those specializing in environmental governance may be inclined to examine the effectiveness of socio-political and economic changes in response to climate change. Further, sociologists may instead tack towards an analysis of the ramifications of the transition on society and on the whole gamut of people's everyday lives while international relations specialists may be interested in understanding how different models of transition – through the process of translation – affect the alignment and power of states at the global level and how this, in turn, impacts on the nature of governance in multilateral settings.

What can be agreed upon is that, for an effective response to climate change to take place, meeting the target set in the Paris Agreement, the scale of the change required is enormous and is likely to recast the relationship between the citizen and the state, the practices of businesses, the power and constraints on nation-states in the international political economy, or potentially, as some suggest, the very economic models and ideologies from which global dependency on the combustion of fossil fuels derives (Klein 2013; Mason 2015). What is more, these changes can be expected to occur in many different ways and not in uniform ways cross-nationally. Thus, the issue of 'translation' becomes a focal topic and is explicated below based on two examples, one from China and one from Japan.

We start with a number of questions. How are the directives or other attempts to socialize environmental ethics from the global level of the United Nations, as a platform of global governance, 'translated' into the grammar of a national polity? How are they communicated to businesses and citizens? How is it made possible within the strictures and power relations within and between states and non-state actors? What is their cultural or ideological impact? What might this mean towards realizing an effective change? And what may this entail for ordinary citizens of a nation in terms of future socio-economic frameworks and governance? The point of translation, here, is to understand in what forms transition is taking place within nation-states or other social systems and, to that end, how change is being communicated (see Rogers 2010: 35). This indeed is no simple task but is nonetheless necessary in order to further understand the processes of social, economic and political developments in a time of enormous global challenges to civilization and fundamental and rapid change, whether the global response to climate change is sufficient for the survival of a tolerable quality of life or not. Upon explaining these general points, the discussion then turns to the contributions this study seeks to make to fill the gap in the existing literature.

There is ample evidence to suggest that both China and Japan are committed to transitioning to renewable energy. We argue that effective **Multi-Sectoral Interaction** (MSI) is an effective means to improve environmental performance and reduce environmental risk. As such, the forging of collaborations and strategic partnerships to maximize social, economic and environmental benefits is essential. To this end, effective communication of environmental management based upon multilateral agreements and international environmental laws is an essential component for the mitigation of environmental risk within a social system (Ji 2018). Of course, a large analytical toolkit deriving from new institutionalism and sociology offers theories of diffusion that demonstrate a number of other elements exist within a social system which aids us in charting the course a polity takes when social systems undergo transition. For instance, rational choice institutionalists may point to the incentive structures placed on agents, historical rules and regularities may be highlighted as constraining forces by historical institutionalists, while the role of cultural norms and socialization on providing pathways for certain types of change over others constitutes a focal point of analysis among sociological institutionalists and sociologists interested in risk management (Schmidt 2008).

Additionally, discursive institutionalists, among others, may emphasize the role of discourse in the process of change (Schmidt 2008) and its link with relational models of diffusion (Wakuta 2015). Moreover, the observation that technologies and governmental strategies of risk management – including the offsetting of responsibility – that proposed solutions to climate risks are reliant upon bear political qualities that impact upon the social lives of citizens (Szerszynski *et al.* 2013; Asayama 2015; Hook *et al.* 2017) brings an additional dimension to the study of social, economic and political change. Without seeking to carry out an exhaustive review of this broad range of research, the point here is to highlight how translation plays an important role in the transition a national polity needs to make to a low carbon or otherwise renewable energy system in a short space of time.

One example of 'translation' is evident in the communication over the roles expected to be played by the public in achieving the Chinese dream in President Xi's speech at the 19th National Congress. As seen above, President Xi's dream purportedly constitutes a form of modernization in which man and nature co-exist harmoniously. The speech represents an admixture of influences from Marxo-Leninism, Maoism, Deng Xiaoping theory, the Three Represents of the CCP but also traditional Chinese philosophy. The discussion here needs to be contextualized by reference to the traditional Confucian conceptions of agency regarding self-cultivation and civic virtue in President Xi's speech. For such conceptions may extend to behavioural adaptations to formulate management strategies to address environmental risk. That is, as Confucius (551–479 BCE) himself proposed, ethical reform towards 'an ethically and ritually disciplined life' (Lai 2008: 19), proposals by President Xi over cultivating social norms to promote realizing the Chinese dream may indeed appeal to the revolutionary sensitivities of party ideology, the relative pragmatism of Deng Xiaoping theory, but also to the traditional conservatism of those with a longer heritage in Chinese politics and elite circles. Of course, such influences are likely to be observable in much of Chinese political thought and discourse.

However, a significant development to emerge from the 19th National Congress was for President Xi's name and political ideas to be written into the party's constitution. Not only that, the Congress granted President Xi his own eponymous school of thought and ideological status, which only the previous leaders Mao Zedong and Deng Xiaoping had accomplished heretofore (Phillips 19 October 2017; Buckley 24 October 2017). President Xi's speech mentioned officially for the first time and detailed Xi Jinping's 'thought on Socialism with Chinese characteristics for a new era' or Xi Jinping theory (*Xi Jinping sixiang*). What role does Xi give to both citizens and businesses to this end?

When the people have faith, the country has power and the nation [*minzu*] has hope. We must improve people's ideological awareness [*sixiang juewu*], moral standards, civilized qualities [*wenming suyang*], and raise the level of civilization of the whole of society. We will launch an extensive education of ideals and faith, deepen publicity and education of socialism with Chinese characteristics and the Chinese dream, carry forward the national spirit and the spirit of the age, strengthen patriotism, collectivism, socialism, and guide people into establishing the correct view of history, national outlook, country and culture. We will implement deeply a citizen morality construction project, promote social ethics, professional ethics, family virtues, individual moral character building, and motivate people to do good, to be filial and concerned about others [*xiaolao aiqin*], to be loyal to the Motherland, and loyal to the people. We will strengthen and improve ideological and political work, and deepen mass activities to build a spiritual civilization.

(*Xinhua* 27 October 2017, our translation)

It is difficult to envisage a leader of a Group of Seven (G7) nation, for instance, making declarations over the reform of social ethics and morality in such a fashion, though the promotion of behavioural change indeed takes place in different forms and is communicated in different ways. Of particular note here is the influence of *li* in Chinese philosophy as a kind of behavioural propriety on social agents influencing the normative codes of conduct in society, and a concept deeply embedded in traditional Chinese philosophy. As opposed to related concepts regarding self-cultivation such as *ren* which loosely relate to a conception of virtue as an innate sense of human interrelatedness and altruistic morality or kindness, *li* focuses on the socialization of norms to guide and constrain – in other words, govern – the inner self (Lai 2008: 26). *Li*, therefore, is observable and can be regulated through people's social conduct. Of course, this is in no way to provide a statement of fact regarding the Confucianist thought underpinning President Xi's speech nor to speculate on the reality of reform once implemented. Rather, the point is to highlight how an 'ecological civilization' and 'spiritual civilization' may be informed by such traditional conceptions of agency within a civic or social domain, in which there is space for the government to discuss implementing a 'citizen morality construction project' and to recrudesce historically situated norms to diverge from current development paths such as promoting a modernization in which 'man and nature' 'co-exist' (*Xinhua* 27 October 2017), a view traceable to traditional Daoist philosophy and far removed from the initial approach to development taken since the establishment of the People's Republic of China in 1949 (Hook *et al.* 2017: 25).

A second example may be seen in the impact of socio-cultural norms at the grassroots level pitted against the vested interests of nuclear power in Japan which are epitomized by the so-called 'nuclear village', a term used to denote pro-nuclear advocates within the government, major companies and academia and their close and powerful relationship with information cartels (Kingston 2013; Hook *et al.* 2017: 37). Japan is heavily reliant on imported gas and oil, largely from a handful of countries in the Middle East and subject to regional competition with China for fossil fuel imports from Russia, and so has championed diversifying sources of gas and oil, risking, at times, damaging its strategic relation with the United States by, for instance, negotiating with Iran over fossil fuel imports (Hook *et al.* 2012: 301–3). To this end, the state and its affiliates within the nuclear village have long promoted nuclear power as a means to overcome vulnerabilities to the nation's energy security as well as for mercantilist reasons. However, anti-nuclear norms emanating from the trauma and collective memory of the two atomic bombs that destroyed the cities of Hiroshima and Nagasaki in August 1945, the harrowing and prolonged social impacts of this, as well as knowledge over large nuclear meltdowns such as the Chernobyl disaster of 1986, intensified as a result of the 3.11 catastrophe. This led to popular opposition which played a prominent role in forcing the shutdown of all fifty nuclear reactors in Japan by September 2013, whose restart depended on passing newly introduced and more rigorous safety guidelines (Kingston 2013), in spite of its effect on electricity prices nationwide. In other words, anti-nuclear norms prevailed, at least temporarily, over the enormous top-down pressure from the nuclear village and their cosy relationship with the main sources of media in Japan (Setouchi *et al.* 2012). This is all the more remarkable because it came with a significant increase of cost to every Japanese household which forced a change in Japanese energy consumption practices.

With this, the Japanese state is promoting wholesale technological innovation to address the issue of environmental (and energy) risk, particularly in the context of 'National Resilience' (*kokudo kyōjin-ka*), a deeply institutionalized initiative which is heavily funded from public and private sectors. As DeWit (2016) points out, in the wake of 3.11, 'building resilience in both the public and private sectors has become explicitly and powerfully linked with renewable energy systems and their enabling storage and transmission technologies', with the core market in National Resilience projected to total between JPY11.8 and 13.5 trillion (at the time of writing, approximately US$105.1–119.3 billion) by 2020. On the one hand, a number of nuclear reactors were restarted as the nuclear lobby has pushed back against popular opposition; on the other, there is abundant evidence that Japan is moving towards renewable energy.

One pertinent example is that the implementation of a feed-in tariff policy in 2011 attracted over 33,000 renewable projects worth approximately US$2 billion in the first few months alone and was led by local banks and credit unions, while citizen cooperation in trialling related innovations appears to have increased following the 3.11 disaster (DeWit 2012, 2013). What are the main drivers of such change? This may be indicative of an 'anthropological shock' over the use of dangerous materials as sources of energy, in which a population who 'feel they have been subjected to a horrendous event', unable to forget its impact, 'will change their future in fundamental and irrevocable ways' (Beck 2015: 79–80). Additionally, there are suggestions that the rapid development of technological innovations related to renewable energies will lead to what Joseph Schumpeter referred to as the 'creative destruction' of old and deeply entrenched economic structures from within; a process which would accelerate market-facilitated responses to climate change and see Japan become a world-leading pioneer of renewable energies (DeWit 2015).

To be clear, creative destruction is a popularized term coined by Austrian economist Joseph Schumpeter which considers technological innovation to be the primary driving-force behind the long-wave cycles of economic expansion to recession originally identified by Russian economist, Nikolai Kondratiev. The central premise for Schumpeter's account is that technological innovation radically transforms the economic system such that old, entrenched economic structures and powers are destroyed and replaced from within. Thus, technological innovation would bring to power new innovators and new enterprises which represent social norms and attitudes different to those of the previously entrenched economic structures that spread across an economic system. Prime Minister Abe, himself, while stating his determination to make Japan the world's 'most innovation-friendly country' (*mottomo inobēshon-o shiyasui kuni*), has suggested Japan would benefit from becoming more Schumpeterian, while referencing Kondratiev waves/cycles at other public speaking events (Abe 6 October 2013, 17 April 2014, 1 May 2014).

The above two examples demonstrate the importance of 'translation' and specifically how transition is communicated. As governments are compelled to follow the metrics set by the UN in responding to climate change, there are varying material factors, governmental mechanisms and unique characteristics of a national polity that can inform the paths of transition to renewable energies and the behavioural adaptation associated with minimizing environmental risk. The example provided for China shows how the state is able to promote, alongside other reforms, a campaign to 'construct' moral codes and ethical practices in the individual directly through political conceptions of a 'sinicized' and historically situated state-socialism that may facilitate, for instance, lifestyle adaptations in response to climate change. Alternatively, the example given for Japan demonstrates the balance of power between an entrenched nuclear lobby and a population heavily impacted by a series of anthropogenic and humanitarian disasters made possible by nuclear technologies. Here, a combination of popular demand and technological development has promoted a market-driven, and technocratic transition (see also DeWit 2017), whether sufficient or not, to renewables with social consciousness over the social risks associated with environmental hazards and energy consumption countering and challenging the previously established view of relying on nuclear power to overcome the vulnerabilities of an over-reliance on fossil fuel imports.

To this end, the approach outlined in this study is developed to contribute to academic inquiry regarding the translation of new models of energy politics, using both China and Japan, two very different social systems, as case studies. Further, by implementing structural equation modelling over the communication of renewable energies and discussion over behavioural change from a variety of media sources, our study develops three empirical models to gauge the influence from main sources of information on industrial users and the mass media, and also examines the MSI between these sources. The governance of environmental risks is often characterized by social complexity which requires debate and deliberation over what is at stake and what choices to make in overcoming the issue while, at the same time, is challenged by complex multilevel, multisectoral and multilateral structures and interactions and scientific uncertainty, particular as regards the speed and exact scale of risk (Gilek *et al.* 2016: 6). Furthermore, it is widely agreed among policymakers, social scientists, civil society organizations and others that effective communication, multi-stakeholder participation and increased involvement of citizens in the processes of deliberation are essential for societies to respond to the effects of climate change and minimize and manage environmental risk (Gilek *et al.* 2016: 9).

This, too, may necessitate changing roles and responsibilities between various stakeholders of a national polity or even within the transnational context. Therefore, the model proposed here contributes a means by which environmental communication is carried out cross-sectorally within a national polity and cross-nationally. It provides three analytical instruments which may be used as social intervention tools for evidence-based policy-making to measure, monitor and intervene over the issue of transitioning to renewable energy. It also proffers empirical measurements of the level of MSI and links these with the EPI, set by the UN as part of the Millennium Development Goals that preceded the SDGs. It is hoped that this tool will offer policymakers and researchers alike a means to assess

MSI among different countries over the diffusion of renewable energies to respond to climate change. Finally, a detailed understanding of the communication of new innovations associated with renewable energy affords researchers further insight into how the directives, targets and norms established by frameworks of global governance are 'translated' by each national polity, and therefore comparative insight into the potential and likely pathways of development cross-nationally. In order to discuss how this was carried out, Chapter 7 explains our research methodology.

6   Multi-sectoral interaction for social diffusion of SDGs

In our efforts to build data-driven empirical models for the translation of the SDGs, we propose three key processes which underline the complex process of the social translation of the SDGs. First is the social communication of SDGs from main sources of information to the public or the social interpreting process. We refer to social actors and agents which have the authorities to interpret and institutionalize the UN SDGs and principles in national contexts and in different domains, for example, governmental agencies, legal organizations, major businesses, top industrial sources, official organizations and research institutes. These social agencies and actors are not directly engaged in the industrial production of goods and commodities or the provision of services to the general public, but they possess the capacity and authority to interpret the abstract principles of the SDGs and adapt the relevant goals and aims within the different national contexts. In our empirical analysis model, we assemble and classify this group of social agencies as the social interpreters of the SDGs. As the corpus analysis shows, different social agents as the SDG interpreters at the national level may adopt different approaches to highlight and interpret specific elements of the sustainable development principles, goals and aims. They play an instrumental role to systematically introduce, adapt and institutionalize the SDGs within specialized domains. For example, governmental agencies may draft governmental reports and official materials such as national development policies and strategic plans based on the social and cultural adaptation of the SDGs. Top industrial bodies and councils may formulate sector-specific policies and regulatory materials to adjust the existing models of industrial operations to realign the priorities with the SDGs. Similarly, research institutes may produce empirical or theoretical research to inform industrial practice and influence policy-making in specialized areas and domains.

The corpus-based empirical analysis focuses to assess the level of inter-action between these social interpreters of the SDGs within each country in terms of the communication of the three key dimensions of the clean energy discourse highlighted in this study, i.e. transition to sustainable lifestyle and associated behaviour changes; production and consumption of sustainable products and services; and the construction of social infrastructure for sustainable development and growth. The inter-sectoral analysis is then extended to the comparison of China and Japan in terms of the level of the inter-sectoral interaction around the social interpretation of the SDGs. It is hypothesized in our study that the higher the level of sectoral interaction in their coverage of the SDGs, the more effective is the social interpretation and communication of the SDGs. Once communicated to the wide society and the intended consumers of the culturally adapted SDGs materials, i.e. national industrial sectors, business entities and the general public, the contextualized and interpreted SDGs goals and principles are implemented and built into concrete managerial procedures and industrial practices. In our empirical corpus analysis, the end-users and consumers of the interpreted SDGs resources are different industrial sectors in the two countries.

Multi-sectoral interaction, cooperation and partnerships development at subnational levels is an under-explored area of study in environmental governance, partly due to the lack of effective analytical models or solid social instruments to gauge and compare the levels of interaction among main institutional agencies of environmental governance. Our study will develop and test the first set of analytical tools to enable cross-national comparative studies of the social diffusion and integration of SDGs related to clean energy consumption and production, social and industrial innovation and lifestyle transition towards sustainable life in China and Japan. We will demonstrate that multi-sectoral interaction can be a powerful intervention mechanism for effective policy-making in tackling environmental risks management issues which require important cross-sectoral collaboration.

The development of the empirical analytical instrument of multi-sectoral interaction will help close gaps in the intra-sectoral understanding and action taking around environmental communication and management among sectoral stakeholders to build much-needed multi-sectoral and cross-national cooperation. The differences between the two countries in terms of multi-sectoral interaction around the social diffusion, culture-specific interpretation and local integration of the principled environmental governance requirements were compared with the widely endorsed global environmental performance index (EPI). The strong alignment between our findings and EPI scores verified the theoretical hypothesis that stronger multi-sectoral interaction at the national level can effectively enhance the overall environmental performance of a country.

How to build effective global governance frameworks to stimulate sectoral, subnational and supranational cooperation around the UN SDGs poses both challenges and opportunities for national and international policymakers. This book pioneers the development of empirical political instruments for the integration of adaptive SDGs in East Asia. The three analytical instruments developed can be used as social intervention tools in evidence-based policy-making to measure, monitor and intervene in the development of new social growth models, with a view to facilitating and enhancing the social diffusion of global SDGs.

Structural equation modelling, also known as path analysis, is a powerful statistical technique widely used in the social sciences. It provides a formalized approach to test theoretical hypotheses regarding the combined effects of two sets of external variables, i.e. independent variables and mediating variables on the observed dependent variables. Our study introduces structural equation modelling to the study of the translation, cultural adaptation and development of the clean/renewable energy generation and consumption discourses in the comparative study of China and Japan as both countries have proactively engaged in transitioning to cleaner and more renewable energy systems, discussed above. This study proposes that an important aspect of the cultural adaptation and diffusion of sustainable development practices conducive to a new energy system is the social accountability attribution process, i.e. the responsibility attached or ascribed to industrial sectors by creditable or authoritative social agencies such as governmental, legislative or industrial regulatory bodies. Three key elements are required to initiate and establish the social accountability attribution, a source of information, a mediating agent and an industrial actor engaged in relevant social and industrial activities. Figure 6.1 illustrates the pathway for the social accountability attribution process which underscores the 'translation' of cultural adaptation and diffusion of renewable energy technologies and practices. This model is distinct from the traditional uni-dimensional model from the source to the intended end-user, as the introduction of the media enables the empirical analysis of its role as a social intervention instrument.

It is hypothesized that the social accountability attributed to industrial sectors is susceptible to both the direct effects from the main sources of information and the indirect effects from the media as a mediating agent. In our study, the term effect is used to describe and gauge the visibility given by sources of information and the media to industrial sectors in discussions of specific aspects and issues related to the production and consumption of renewable energy in national contexts. More specifically, the level of sectoral visibility is gauged through the frequency analysis of industrial sectors in materials published by different sources of information such as governmental

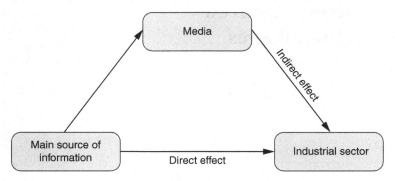

Figure 6.1 Path analysis of the cultural adaptation and diffusion of clean/renewable energy discourses.

agencies, industrial sources, business sources and by mediating agencies such as newspapers and journals and magazines. The corpus analysis demonstrates that in the social diffusion of renewable energy discourses, as part of the 'translation' process, different sources of information in the two countries play distinct roles in engaging with different industrial sectors regarding the production and utilization of renewable energies. The mediating variables included in the corpus study, i.e. newspapers and magazines/journals, can significantly improve the predictive power of the structural equation model. The mass media plays a dynamic role in moderating the transmission of renewable energy discourses from different sources of information, e.g. government, business, top industrial bodies to industrial sectors. This study provides empirical evidence on the role of the mass media as a social intervention that can be influenced and influence the level of public visibility of specific industrial sectors. As per the theoretical approach, outlined above, this is applicable to the diffusion of environmental norms in order to attain SDGs in China and Japan.

7 Corpus research methodologies

This chapter explicates our research methodology in designing and implementing structural equation modelling to discourses on renewable energies. It is separated into two sections. The first explains the data collection process while the second provides a detailed overview of the interpretation of the model created and constructs the research hypothesis. As discussed at the outset of the study, we propose, illustrate and test three social mechanisms which underscore the diffusion of sustainable discourses in China and Japan. These are addressed below following a suitable explanation of the basis of our research methodology. That is, on how the data were collected and organized as well as the design and considerations behind the overall model proposed based on structural equation modelling. Given the extensiveness of our overall model, a composite of three empirical models, the subsequent chapters also provide some methodological considerations for each of the three proposed social mechanisms for better clarity. In other words, this chapter charts the course taken in collecting and organizing the data and designing the overall model to be tested, the results of which are discussed in the subsequent chapters.

Before introducing the concept and explaining the process of building multi-sectoral interaction as a social intervention to foster the development of the sustainable living and growth discourse, we will explain the research design which underlines the statistical configuration and the subsequent empirical analysis of the relationships between different social actors. The Factiva database provides a comprehensive search interface which allows the retrieval of text data within a certain set parameter. The specification of the scope of the automatic retrieval of the corpus text materials rests upon the aim of the corpus research. If the aim of using the digital corpus is to find out and compare the reporting of a particular dimension of the sustainable living and consumption discourse by different social source of information or communication agents in either China or Japan, we input the topic-specific query string in Chinese or Japanese into the free text search area of the Factiva interface, and set the corpus mining parameters to narrow down the search to a specific time period, source of information by social sector, the language of the publications and, finally, the geographical location. For example, one can extract and compare the frequencies of occurrence of database articles pertinent to the transition to sustainable lifestyle and related behaviour change which are published by Chinese official, governmental, legal, business and research sources on a yearly basis. The frequency data can be then used for correlation analyses such as Spearman's correlation test to find out the level of similarity or dissimilarity between sources of information or social communication agents.

All data were collated from the Factiva database (Dow Jones 2017), a global news database consisting of a wide-range of licensed and free publications in numerous languages including Traditional and Simplified Chinese script and Japanese. The database includes a large range of licensed digital materials published by governmental, industrial and business sources in different countries in their original languages since the mid-1990s. Chinese and Japanese data were collected separately. For data collection in Chinese, both traditional and simplified scripts were selected and mainland China was the geographical parameter; for data collection in Japanese, only sources from Japan in Japanese were included. First, the terms for 'clean energy' (Chinese: *qingjie nengyuan*; Japanese: *kurīn enerugī*) and 'renewable energy' (Chinese: *kezaisheng nengyuan*; Japanese: *saisei kanō enerugī*) were input into the search engine. Here, based on a reading of both Chinese and Japanese data, three expressions were used to retrieve data on lifestyle changes and societal change, the focal topic in this study. These were 'way of life' (Chinese: *shenghuo fangshi*; Japanese: *ikikata*), 'awareness' (Chinese: *yishi*; Japanese: *ishiki*) and 'behaviour' (Chinese: *xingwei*; Japanese: *kōdō*). These terms were then used in a new search which was constructed in Chinese and Japanese separately as follows: '(clean energy or renewable energy) and (way of life or awareness or behaviour).

This meant that either or both of the energy terms and at least one of the 'lifestyle' terms must occur in the same article for it to be included in the search output. Following this, based on the total number of publications that were output, fifty articles were selected using a random number generator. Two word lists, one in Chinese and one in Japanese, were compiled based on a careful reading of the fifty articles for each language respectively where words denoting lifestyle changes and visions for a new society were extracted. This exact process was repeated for words denoting forms of 'infrastructure' and 'products', too. Once the word list of words denoting lifestyle change or visions for a new social model or form of social organization (e.g. a 'smart city') were compiled, the frequency of each individual term in both lists was retrieved by carrying out new searches on Factiva as follows: '(clean energy or renewable energy) and Term X'.

Once the frequencies were retrieved, the 40–50 (China: 44; Japan: 41) most frequently used terms were selected to form a new word list denoting lifestyle change and visions for a new society. These lists are provided in Appendices 1 and 2. It is important to note that, up to this point, all searches used exactly the same terms in Chinese and Japanese. However, at this stage, we had compiled a Chinese and a Japanese word list which were not identical but instead were meant to better reflect both corpora respectively. A series of searches were then made to retrieve information regarding business sources and industrial sectors, using the form: '(clean energy or renewable energy) and (term a or term b or term c or ... term x)', where the terms in the second parentheses comprise the 40–50 most frequently used terms of the new word list denoting changes in lifestyle, social vision and social organizations. For these searches, a time parameter was set from 1 January 2000 to the present day (September 2017) while all other parameters remained the same as above. From this, the annual frequency of articles from Business Sources, Governmental Sources, Magazines and Journals, Newspapers and Top Industry Sources were collated and separated by source. Searching for each industrial sector individually, the frequency per year of articles pertaining to lifestyle change or visions of a new society was retrieved for the following industrial sectors, separately:

- Agriculture
- Automotive
- Basic Materials and Resources
- Business and Consumer Services
- Consumer Goods
- Financial Services
- Healthcare and Life Science
- Industrial Goods
- Leisure/Arts/Hospitality
- Media/Entertainment
- Real Estate/Construction
- Retail/Wholesale
- Technology
- Telecommunications Services
- Transportation and Logistics
- Utilities

Additionally, the industrial sector 'Energy Total' was expanded and the frequencies for the following energy sectors were collated:

• Alternative Fuels
• Nuclear Fuel

While Natural Gas is included among sectors within 'Energy Total', it was excised from the analysis as no sources in Japanese came under this section, despite being the largest global importer of LNG. All frequencies were then tabulated and organized for the statistical tests we subsequently carried out.

The development of the parallel bilingual terminology in Chinese and Japanese provides a useful tool to study and compare the two countries in terms of the social diffusion and communication of the clean energy discourse in three inter-related dimensions: construction of infrastructure for the production of renewable energy; products and services using renewable energy; and individual lifestyle and behaviour change. In the following sections, we will analyse the interaction and relationships between different social actors and sectoral agents which all contribute to the growing clean energy discourse and consumption cultures in China and Japan. These include governmental agencies, businesses, legal organizations and research institutes as the identified main stakeholders in the social construction and diffusion of the sustainable living and development discourse. Three large sets of sustainability terminologies were compiled for Chinese and Japanese resources: lifestyle and behaviour change; products and services using renewable energy; infrastructure for the production of renewable energy.

8 Sustainable living discourse in China

In order to illustrate the linguistic, cultural and knowledge translation process which underscores the transition towards sustainable society in China, this study investigates the development of the sustainable environmental and living discourse (SELD) in the country and builds empirical analytical models to explore the impact of the language translation and knowledge translation strata on the rise of SELD in China since early 2000s. Important patterns emerged from the corpus analysis which supported the theoretical hypothesis regarding the dual translation mechanism of the social communication and local adaptation of sustainability. That is, the growth of SELD is propelled and driven by both innovation in the language translation of sustainability and the socially embedded and contextualized interpretation of sustainability principles by a range of information sources or also known as the social interpreting agents of sustainability (SIAs) in this study.

Global governance through goal setting differs significantly from approaches such as rule-making or norm promotion in that it requires the development of and experiment with a new set of political intervention instruments and social mechanisms to enable the effective diffusion and local integration of adaptive SDGs in national contexts. This study argues that in order to facilitate and optimize the social dissemination and uptake of the UN SDGs, it is methodologically feasible and productive to integrate insights from translation studies and media communication into the patterns and dynamics of the utilization of translated sustainability terminologies across society over time. This study offers a corpus-based linguistic analysis of the translation and communication of SELD as a topic-specific genre of the general sustainability discourse in China between 2000 and 2018. It will explore the social communication and utilization of translated sustainability terminology in China to illustrate the unique features, patterns and mechanisms of the growth of the sustainability discourse in China, as well as the wide implications of this case study for the emerging interdisciplinary research field of sustainability translation in general. The corpus linguistic analysis of a rich body of digitalized Chinese sustainability materials will focus to address three key interrelated research questions:

1. Regarding the language translation of sustainability, how has translated sustainability terminologies or specifically, the SELD terminology been communicated, socially disseminated and culturally adapted within the Chinese social and cultural system in the last two decades?
2. At the level of the knowledge translation of sustainability, what are the social interpreting agents of sustainability principle, values and idea sets in China, and whether and how do these social interpreting agents interact with each other to foster environmental culture, raise social awareness and build consensus and shared understanding around sustainable living and citizens' responsibilities?
3. Within the proposed dual sustainability translation process or mechanism, whether and how do the language translation and the knowledge translation processes interact with each other and show consistent patterns over time?

At the *language translation* level, the Chinese digital corpus analysis shows that the introduction of SDGs has given rise to not only a large number of new translated terminologies, but also an array of highly innovative and locally designed sustainability expressions that have significantly enriched the evolving sustainability discourse in China. Effective and socially contextualized language translation of sustainability plays an instrumental role to facilitate and enable the public understanding and the subsequent voluntary compliance with and endorsement of abstract SDGs principles, values and idea sets at the national and local levels. Through quantitative corpus analyses, this study attempts to establish the relations between the introduction and social communication of translated sustainability terminologies and the patterns of the growth of the discourse of sustainable living and citizens' responsibilities of environmental protection.

At the *knowledge translation* level, this study will explore the process in which translated SDGs are diffused across the society and communicated to the general public within the twenty year time span between 2000 and 2018. Current translation studies have rarely touched upon the mechanism of the social communication and diffusion of translated sustainability information in the target language and cultural system, especially through formalized linguistic analyses. To fill in this research gap, this study will introduce quantitative social diffusion models from sociology (Hagerstrand 1967; Cavalli-Sforza and Feldman 1980; Mahajan and Peterson 1985; McAdam and Rucht 1993) to the emerging field of sustainability translation in particular, and socially orientated empirical translation studies in general.

Large amounts of original Chinese sustainability publications were used to construct formalized models of the social dissemination of translated terminology in the Chinese society since the turn of the twenty-first century. The empirical analytical models help illustrate the varying contributions of sustainability information diffusion agents to the knowledge base and shared understanding of sustainability in China. The models thus constructed provide insights into the patterns of the interaction and dynamics among social sectors around sustainability communication and social promotion. The rising sustainability discourse affords an important opportunity of inter-sectoral interaction and engagement which underscore growing social movements in China that may be broadly termed as the green revolution or the rise of the green generation.

It is hypothesized that the social diffusion of translated environmental terminologies and associated locally designed expressions is facilitated by a social diffusion network. The network encompasses a range of sustainability interpreting agents (SIAs) which have the authority to interpret and adapt abstract SDGs and related principles and concepts within their sectoral confines. Typical SIAs which make up the social diffusion network are governmental agencies, legal institutions, business entities, research bodies, top industrial organizations, etc. These social actors can interpret sustainability goals and aims within the remit of their sectoral responsibility; and, more importantly, translate the concepts and principles of sustainability into practices using available sectoral and local resources. The quantitative corpus analysis demonstrates that these SIAs make varying contributions to the growth of the sustainable living and citizens' responsibility discourse.

Growing sustainable living discourse in China

All data were collated from the Factiva database (Dow Jones 2017), a global news database consisting of a wide-range of licensed and free publications in numerous languages including Chinese. The database includes a large range of licensed digital materials published by governmental, industrial and business sources in different countries in their original languages since the mid-1990s. Based on the exploration of the digital Chinese publications, four large groups of terms were extracted which are closely related to sustainable living and citizens' social responsibilities to protect their living and working environments. The four large word categories encompass translations from original English terms and a number of locally designed expressions representing useful efforts to adapt abstract

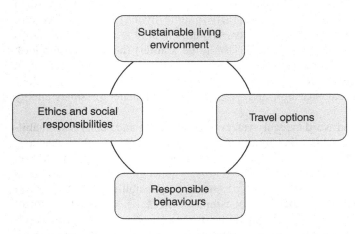

Figure 8.1 Word categories of sustainable living and citizens' social responsibilities.

sustainability principles and goals into concrete and specific actions and behaviours. The four word categories highlighted are responsible behaviours; green ethics and social responsibilities for sustainability; green and sustainable living environments; and green or sustainable transport and travel options. These four sets of sustainability terminologies were used to query the database and extract frequency data of publications on particular topics and dimensions of promoting green living style and the public awareness of sustainability. It is hypothesized that the acceptance and circulation of these translated terminologies by different social agencies may have an impact on the sustainability discourse in China.

The first word category is defined sustainable consumption behaviour: 光盘行动 (guāngpán xíngdòng) (eat-it-up campaign, to avoid food waste); 理性消费 (lǐxìng xiāofèi) (rational consumption); 新文化消费 (xīn wénhuà xiāofèi) (consumption based on new cultures); 低碳消费 (dī tàn xiāofèi) (low-carbon consumption) 低碳消费 行为 (dī tàn xiāofèi xíngwéi) (low carbon consumption behaviour); 理性购买行为 (lǐxìng gòumǎi xíngwéi) (rational purchase behaviour); 过度消费 (guòdù xiāofèi) (over-consumption); 环境行为 (huánjìng xíngwéi) (environmental behaviour); 环境教育 (huánjìng jiàoyù) (environmental education); 节水 (jié shuǐ) (water saving); 节能 (jiénéng) (energy saving); 节能量 (jié néngliàng) (amount of energy saved/conserved); 节能降耗 (jiénéng jiànghào) (energy saving and consumption reduction); 家庭使用 (jiātíng shǐyòng) (family use); 节俭用餐 (jiéjiǎn yòngcān) (thrifty dining); 可持续消费 (kěchíxù xiāofèi) (sustainable consumption); 科学消费 (kēxué xiāo fèi) (scientific consumption); 垃圾分类 (lājī fēnlèi) (waste classification); 铅回收 (qiān huíshōu) (lead recycling); 清洁利用 (qīngjié lìyòng) (clean utilization); 省 电 (shěng diàn) (electricity saving); 消费行为 (xiāofèi xíngwéi) (consumption behaviour); 自家消费 (zìjiā xiāofèi) (home consumption); 自给自足 (zìjǐ zìzú) (self-sufficient); 自我负担 (zìwǒ fùdān) (self-pay); 责任消费 (zérèn xiāofèi) (responsible consumption); 汽车共享 (qìchē gòngxiǎng) (car sharing); and 智慧节能 (zhìhuì jiénéng) (smart energy saving).

The second word category refers to green ethics and social responsibilities for sustainability in Chinese: 碳贞操 (tàn zhēncāo) (carbon chastity); 低碳使命 (dī tàn shǐmìng) (low-carbon mission); 生态文明 (shēng tài wén míng) (ecological civilization); 生态力量 (shēngtài lìliàng) (ecological power); 社会责任 (shèhuì zérèn) (social responsibility); 社会 责 任感 (shèhuì zérèngǎn) (social responsibility); 道德 选择 (dàodé xuǎnzé) (moral choice); 环境责任 (huánjìng zérèn) (environmental responsibilities); 环保意识 (huánbǎo yìshí) (awareness of environmental protection); 环境伦理 (huánjìng lúnlǐ) (environmental ethics); 环境贡献 (huánjìng gòngxiàn) (environmental contribution); 价值观 (jiàzhíguān) (values); 价值取向 (jiàzhí qǔxiàng) (value orientation); 生 产者延伸责任 (shēngchǎn zhě yánshēn zérèn) (extended producer responsibility); 企业社会责任 (qǐyè shèhuì zérèn) (corporate social responsibility); 社会公共利益 (shèhuì gōnggòng lìyì) (social public interests); 诚信经 营 (chéngxìn jīngyíng) (business integrity); 消费者态度 (xiāofèi zhě tàidù) (consumer attitude) and 意识改革 (yìshí gǎigé) (awareness reform).

The third word category is green living environment which broadly includes built environments, communities, schools, future city design and sustainable lifestyle: 百年住宅 (bǎinián zhùzhái) (centennial residence, with energy-efficient and sustainable design); 低碳校园 (dī tàn xiàoyuán) (low-carbon campus); 低碳乡村 (dī tàn xiāngcūn) (low-carbon village); 低碳社区 (dī tàn shèqū) (low-carbon community); 低碳家庭 (dī tàn jiātíng) (low-carbon family); 绿色生活 (lùsè shēnghuó) (green life); 零碳生活 (líng tàn shēnghuó) (zero-carbon life); 绿 色校园 (lùsè xiàoyuán) (green campus); 绿色设施 (lùsè shèshī) (green facilities); 生态村 (shēngtài cūn) (eco-village); 生态城区 (shēngtài chéngqū) (eco-city); 生态生活 (shēngtài shēnghuó) (eco-life); 生态住宅 (shēngtài zhùzhái) (ecological residence); 生态城市 (shēngtài chéngshì) (eco-cities); 低碳城市 (dī tàn chéngshì) (low-carbon cities); 低碳建筑 (dī tàn jiànzhú) (low-carbon building); 低碳生活 (dī tàn shēnghuó) (low-carbon life); 低碳环境 (dī tàn huánjìng) (low-carbon environment); 海绵城市 (hǎimián chéngshì) (sponge city); 可再生能 源建筑 (kě zàishēng néngyuán jiànzhù) (renewable energy building); 绿色建筑 (lùsè jiànzhù) (green building); 湿地公园 (shīdì gōngyuán) (wetland park); 消费生活 (xiāofèi shēnghuó) (consumption life); 永续家园 (yǒng xù jiāyuán) (sustainable home); 智慧家庭 (zhìhuì jiātíng) (smart families); 智慧城市 (zhìhuì chéngshì) (smart cities); 智能家居 (zhìnéng jiājū) (smart homes); 城市环境 (chéngshì huánjìng) (urban environment); 垂直绿化 (chuízhí lǜhuà) (vertical greening); 持续环境 (chíxù huánjìng) (sustainable environment); 无废城市 (wú fèi chéngshì) (waste-less city); 智慧社区 (zhìhuì shèqū) (smart communities); 智能城市 (zhìnéng chéngshì) (intelligent cities); and 智能生活 (zhìnéng shēnghuó) (intelligent life).

The last word category studied is green transport and travel options which include high-frequency words such as 共享单车 (gòngxiǎng dānchē) (shared bike); 绿色交通 (lǜsè jiāotōng) (green traffic); 零碳交通 (líng tàn jiāotōng) (zero carbon transportation); 绿色快递 (lǜsè kuàidì) (green express); 智能物流 (zhìnéng wùliú) (smart logistics); 多式联运 (duō shì liányùn) (multimodal transport); 低碳交通 (dī tàn jiāotōng) (low-carbon transportation); 慢行系统 (màn xíng xìtǒng) (slow transportation system); 智能快递 (zhìnéng kuàidì) (smart express); 磁悬浮 (cíxuánfú) (Maglev); 磁悬浮列车 (cíxuánfú lièchē) (Maglev trains); 无碳交通 (wú tàn jiāotōng) (carbon-free traffic); 运输路径 (yùnshū lùjìng) (transport paths); 自动驾驶 (zìdòng jiàshǐ) (autopilot); 智慧交通 (zhìhuì jiāotōng) (smart transport); 低碳出行 (dī tàn chūxíng) (low-carbon travel); 零碳出行 (líng tàn chūxíng) (zero-carbon travel); and 微旅行 (wēi lǚxíng) (mini trips or short, low-cost trips).

The generalised linear regression model (GLRM) is widely used in social sciences to explore the relations between a set of explanatory factors and the dependence variable. It is an extension of the ordinary least squares (OLS) regression which assumes the distribution of the dependence variable data to be normal. This study uses GLRM to model the relations between three external factors, i.e. sustainability interpreting agents (SIA), sustainability word categories (SWC) and the year of publication (YOP). SIA refers to social agents who interpret and adapt locally the abstract principles, idea sets and values of translated sustainability concepts and expressions in the Chinese cultural and social context. For the purposes of illustrating the empirical or formalized analytical models, six social agents which assume the social functions of interpreting, communicating, localizing and promoting translated sustainability goals, principles and values were highlighted in the corpus analysis of Chinese digitalized publications on sustainable living and social transition: business sources; official reports; government and political sources; legal sources; major business news sources; and top industrial sources.

The sectoral classification framework mirrors the structure of the Factiva database. Publications from these sources are intended mainly for specialized audiences with knowledge of and interests in materials that are

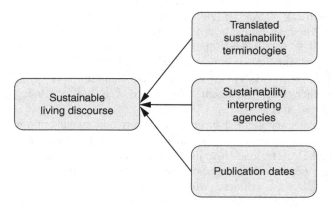

Figure 8.2 GLRM model.

relevant and significant for their particular sectors, for example, official briefs, governmental and administrative materials, or business and industrial news for professionals. It is hypothesized that the engagement of these sources of information plays an important role in the process of translating, adapting sustainability principles and values in the local context. Using these sources of information in the GLRM can help identify and analyse the relative contributions of these distinct sectors to the discussions around sustainable living and lifestyle change in China over the last twenty years.

The second explanatory variable included in the GLRM construction is sustainability word categories. The last external explanatory variable included in the GLRM is the publication date within the time span of 2000 and 2018. Relevant publication data before 2000 are less than sufficient to build and compare alternative hypotheses using the GLRM. Statistically significant relationships between these sectoral sustainability interpreters are described as multi-sectoral interaction. For example, when using *generalized linear regression* models to fit and predict publications on sustainability in the large digital database used in this study, if the regression coefficients of the independent variables, i.e. the social interpreting agents of sustainability are shown to make contributions in the same direction, multi-sectoral interaction is said to exist among these social actors in their function of the socially embedded interpretation and communication of sustainability goals and principles within the importing culture and society. Alternatively, if the regression models detect differences between the social actors in terms of the direction of their respective regression coefficients, some lack of multi-sectoral interaction among this group of social interpreters of sustainability, or at least the disengagement of those attributed with negative coefficient scores from the others is ascertained. Higher multi-sectoral interaction provides stronger and better focused social communication network for the effective diffusion of sustainability. Lack of interaction with and engagement of certain sectors can weaken the cross-sectoral consensus and cooperation.

Impact of language and knowledge translation

This section will explore the impact of the language and knowledge translation processes on the development and wide social diffusion of the sustainable living and lifestyle change discourse in China between 2000 and 2018. Specifically, the formalized corpus linguistic analysis will examine whether there is any statistically significant relation between the hypothesized explanatory factors, i.e. different word categories of translated sustainability terminology and the six social interpreting agents promoting the social communication of sustainability and the dependent variable which is the growth in the publication of sustainable living related materials and resources in China in the last two decades. In this section, the analysis of the impact from the dual translation process is carried out separately, and the next section examines the impact of the interaction between the two processes on the growing social importance of the sustainable living discourse.

Table 8.1 shows that all of the three explanatory factors, SIA, SWC and YOP have significant impact on the dependent variable which is the publications on sustainable living from various social communication channels. SIA, SWC and YOP are categorical independent variables, and the dependent variable Publications of Sustainable Living is a continuous variable. SIA has six levels ranging from business, governmental to legal

Table 8.1 Generalized linear regression model (GLRM) tests of model effects

Source	Type III		
	Wald chi-square	*Df*	*Sig.*
(Intercept)	340.047	1	*
Sustainability Interpreting Agents (SIA)	135.819	6	*
Sustainability Word Categories (SWC)	160.066	3	*
Publication Year (YOP)	225.484	18	*

Note
p values were too low to fit in this table. Therefore, statistically significant p values as smaller than 0.05 (two-tailed) are indicated by an asterisk.

sources of information; SWC has four levels referring to four dimensions of the translated terminology of sustainable living which are environmental social behaviour; green ethics and social responsibilities; sustainable community and built environment; and green travel options. Lastly, YOP encloses the two decades between 2000 and 2018. It is necessary to examine variations in the contribution to sustainable living discourse among different levels within each of the three independent variables. This requires the computation of parameter estimates which break the total effect from each independent variable down to each of its component level.

Table 8.2 shows that except for major business news sources, five of the six main sources of information as sustainability interpreting agents have significant impact on the dependent variable ($p < 0.05$). The largest explanatory factor is Business Sources. The regression coefficient B for this source of information is 468, which suggests that with the increase of one unit in the independent variable, i.e. one business source of information, there is an increase of 468 publications on sustainable living in the Chinese materials included in the Factiva database. This is followed by Official Reports which has a regression coefficient of 341, indicating that with the increase of one official source of information or report, there is an increase of 341 publications on sustainable living in the same database. To a less extent, Legal Sources and Major Business News Sources also contribute to the growth of the sustainable living discourse over the same time span, i.e. from 2000 to 2018. However, the level of contribution from Major Business News Sources is not statistically significant to be included in the GLRM. Top Industrial Sources has been attributed a negative regression coefficient score indicating the disengagement of this social interpreting agency in discussions of transition towards sustainable lifestyle and society building. The lack of alignment of Top Industrial Sources with other sources of information detects a gap in the hypothesized sectoral interaction between social interpreting agents around promoting and building shared social consensus and understanding of sustainability as a priority in socio-economic development.

Table 8.3 shows that with the exception of green transportation and travel alternatives, three of the four categories of the translated sustainability terminology have important contributions to the growing sustainable living discourse in China. The largest contributor or the most significant topic of discussion is the word category of environmentally responsible behaviour with a regression coefficient of 427, suggesting that with the increase of one unit in the independent variable, i.e. reporting regarding environmentally responsible behaviour, there is an increase of as many as 427 publications related to this topic in the Chinese publications

Table 8.2 GLRM parameter estimates: Sustainability Interpreting Agents (SIA) as IV

Sustainability Interpreting Agents	B	Std. error	95% Wald confidence interval		Hypothesis test		
			Lower	Upper	Wald chi-square	df	Sig.
Business sources	468.179	49.5690	371.026	565.333	89.208	1	*
Official reports	341.455	49.5690	244.302	438.609	47.451	1	*
Government and political sources	336.521	49.5690	239.368	433.675	46.090	1	*
Legal sources	244.626	49.5690	147.473	341.780	24.355	1	*
Major business news	65.271	49.5690	−31.882	162.425	1.734	1	0.188
Top industrial sources	−425.031	70.0983	−562.421	−287.641	36.764	1	*

Note
All significant p values were too low to fit in this table. Therefore, statistically significant p values as smaller than 0.05 (two-tailed) are indicated by an asterisk.

Table 8.3 GLRM parameter estimates: Sustainability Word Categories (SWC) as IV

| Word category | B | Std. error | 95% Wald confidence interval | | Hypothesis test | | |
			Lower	Upper	Wald chi- square	df	Sig.
Environmentally responsible behaviour	427.260	37.4669	353.827	500.694	130.044	1	*
Green ethics and social responsibilities	312.584	37.4669	239.150	386.017	69.605	1	*
Green living environment	107.388	37.4669	33.954	180.822	8.215	1	*
Green transportation and travel options	32.429	34.3265	−34.850	99.707	892	1	0.345

Note
Many *p* values were too low to fit in this table. Therefore, statistically significant *p* values as smaller than 0.05 (two-tailed) are indicated by an asterisk.

of the Factiva database. Typical examples of translated terms and locally created expressions related to environmentally responsible behaviours include: thrifty dining; sustainable consumption; scientific consumption; waste classification; clean utilization; save electricity; self-consumption; self-sufficient; self-pay; and responsible consumption. The second largest contributing factor is sustainability terms related to green ethics and social responsibilities and duties. The regression coefficient for this level of SWC is 321, which means that with the increase of one unit in this variable, i.e. green ethics and social responsibilities, there is an increase of 321 publications across the six sources of information in the Factiva database. The third dimension of the translated sustainability terminology which contributes significantly to the sustainable living discourse is green living environment such as the design of sustainable built environment. Typical translated and localized terms in this category are millennium housing; low-carbon village; low-carbon community; low-carbon family; green campus; green facility; eco-village; eco-city; eco-life; and ecological residence. Some terms in this category refer to abstract concepts such as sustainable community and broader social environment favourable of sustainable lifestyle. The statistical result suggests that there is not enough interest on green travel options ($p=0.345>0.05$) across the six social interpreting agents.

Table 8.4 shows that the sustainable living discourse saw significant growth only after 2010. Two thousand and eleven is the first year when the rate of growth of publications discussing the four dimensions of sustainability reached a statistically significant level. Important environmental events in China in 2011 include the publication of the carbon dioxide emission reduction and energy saving legislation as part of the twelfth five-year plan which started in 2011. In this momentous and legally binding regulation, two ambitious emission reduction targets were added which were the country's consumption of non-fossil fuels to reach an overall level of 11.4 per cent; and a reduction of 17 per cent in carbon dioxide emission per every GDP. This was the first time that the Chinese government officially treated carbon dioxide emission as an integral part of the assessment of the performance of local, provincial and central governmental administrations. Internationally, the Great East Japan earthquake and tsunami trigged the Fukushima nuclear disaster. This caused much concern and heated debates among the public about food and water safety issues, and a growing public awareness of the importance of a sustainable living style, and less dependence on energies that may cause severe environmental problems. Prior to that, only the year 2007 saw important growth of publications on sustainable living, which was the year before the 2008 Beijing Summer Olympics.

Table 8.4 GLRM parameter estimates: Year of Publication (YOP) as IV

Year of publication	B	Std. error	95% Wald confidence interval		Hypothesis test		
			Lower	Upper	Wald chi-square	df	Sig.
[Year=2018]	470.893	81.6461	310.869	630.916	33.264	1	*
[Year=2017]	756.893	81.6461	596.869	916.916	85.940	1	*
[Year=2016]	505.929	81.6461	345.905	665.952	38.398	1	*
[Year=2015]	457.429	81.6461	297.405	617.452	31.389	1	*
[Year=2014]	304.107	81.6461	144.084	464.131	13.873	1	*
[Year=2013]	290.242	80.9508	131.582	448.903	12.855	1	*
[Year=2012]	292.628	82.4118	131.104	454.153	12.608	1	*
[Year=2011]	312.429	81.6461	152.405	472.452	14.643	1	*
[Year=2010]	154.750	81.6461	−5.273	314.773	3.592	1	0.058
[Year=2009]	99.643	81.6461	−60.381	259.666	1.489	1	0.222
[Year=2008]	111.714	81.6461	−48.309	271.738	1.872	1	0.171
[Year=2007]	**163.607**	**81.6461**	**3.584**	**323.631**	**4.015**	**1**	*
[Year=2006]	160.000	81.6461	−0.023	320.023	3.840	1	0.050
[Year=2005]	116.786	81.6461	−43.238	276.809	2.046	1	0.153
[Year=2004]	46.750	81.6461	−113.273	206.773	0.328	1	0.567
[Year=2003]	28.393	81.6461	−131.631	188.416	0.121	1	0.728
[Year=2002]	42.714	81.6461	−117.309	202.738	0.274	1	0.601
[Year=2001]	12.429	81.6461	−147.595	172.452	0.023	1	0.879
[Year=2000]	16.500	72.0162	−124.649	157.649	0.052	1	**0.819**

Note
Most signicant *p* values were too low to fit in this table. Therefore, statistically significant *p* values as smaller than 0.05 (two-tailed) are indicated by an asterisk.

Impact of the interaction of language and knowledge translation

The GLRM has so far focused on the relations between the individual independent variable and the dependent variable. It was found that while all of the three independent variables have significant impact on the growth of the sustainable living discourse in China, contributions from different levels of the three independent variables do vary. For example, within the explanatory variable of Sustainability Interpreting Agents (SIAs), Top Industrial Sources have proved to be least engaged in discussions of sustainable living, whereas the other five SIAs have been actively contributing to the interpretation and adaptation of sustainability ethics, principles and idea sets within their sectoral contexts. For example, the SIA which has contributed most to the sustainable living discourse in China is Business Sources. This is followed by Official Reports, Governmental and Political Sources; and to a lesser extent, Legal Sources.

Within the independent variable of Translated Sustainability Terminology, the word categories of Environmentally Responsible Behaviour and Green Ethics and Social Responsibilities have provided the foci of the discourse of transition to sustainable living in China. It is worth noting that a number of expressions compiled into these two sustainability term categories represent important local adaptation and enrichment of the original English sustainability terminology. Expressions such as eat-it-up campaign (to avoid food waste typically seen in Chinese business banquets); thrifty dining; new civilized consumption; self-sufficient; carbon chastity; ecological civilization; awareness reform are fully embedded in the Chinese culture and social context. Green Living Environment, especially with regard to the development of green communities and sustainable built environment, constitutes another key dimension of the sustainability living discourse in China. Lastly, the corpus data show that Green Transportation Options represents an underrepresented area across the diverse sources of information under study.

The yearly distribution data reveal interesting and convincing patterns regarding the wide social promotion of sustainable living in China. Prior to 2011, the growth of publications in this area was rather limited, as there was no significant relation between the independent variable of publication dates and the total volume of publications. The only exception was 2007, the year before the 2008 Beijing Summer Olympics which saw a sudden peak in discussion around sustainable lifestyle and environmental protection. More consistent patterns of the increase in sustainable living and consumption publications were established in the statistical analysis of the corpus data from 2011, another year of major international and domestic environmental events. Internally, the central government published the twelfth five-year plan for the period between 2011 and 2015 which incorporated for the first carbon dioxide emission reduction in the overall evaluation of performance of local, regional and central administrations.

This section explores the effects or impact of the interaction between the dual translation processes on the introduction, translation and development of the sustainable living discourse in China. This is based on the hypothesis that the interpretation and adaptation of sustainability principles and values by sectors or social interpreting agents (SIAs) may exhibit contrastive or complementary patterns as a result of the sectoral priorities of SIAs for specific dimensions of the sustainability discourse. For example, it is suspected that industrial agents or sources of information may display less interest in topics such as sustainability ethics and responsible consumption behaviour than government and political sources of information. By contrast, major business and industrial interpreting agencies may show stronger interests in promoting sustainable lifestyle such as green travel options in social systems where sustainability innovation is led by industrial or business sectors, instead of governmental agents. Better alignment across sources of information or SIAs in a country in terms of the sectoral interpretation and investment in the sustainable living discourse may serve as an indication of the existence of multisectoral interaction which may provide a more favourable and conducive social environment for cross-sectoral cooperation around sustainable development and social transition. By contrast, if the SIAs within a country exhibit distinct patterns of the sectoral engagement with the sustainable living discourse with minimal interaction among the SIAs under study, the disparity thus identified may pose challenges to cross-sectoral partnership around the translation and social adaptation of sustainability principles and values in the national context.

Interaction between Sustainability Interpreting Agents (SIA) and Sustainability Word Categories (SWC)

The statistical results of the GLRM reported in this section show the effects on the development of the sustainable living discourse of the interaction between different levels of SIAs, i.e. the six social interpreting agencies and the four levels of Sustainability Word Categories (SWC), i.e. the four dimensions of sustainable living highlighted in this study. The patterns identified in this section provide useful insights into the sectorally motivated engagement with the sustainable living discourse in China across the six SIAs for the period under investigation, i.e. between 2000 and 2018, especially over the last ten years when the introduction and adaptation of sustainability principles, values and idea sets evolved gradually from a peripheral position to a key item in the social and economic agenda of the country.

Table 8.5 shows that the Chinese business sector is more engaged in the discussion of environmentally responsible social behaviour and green

Table 8.5 Interaction between SIA and SWC: SIA = Business Sources

Interaction between Social Interpreting Agencies and Sustainability Word Category	B	Std. error	95% Wald confidence interval		Hypothesis test		
			Lower	Upper	Wald chi-square	df	Sig.
[Business source] & [Word Category = Behaviour]	992.89	112.163	773.058	1212.73	78.362	1	*
[Business source] & [Word Category = Ethics]	662.84	112.163	443.006	882.679	34.923	1	*
[Business source] & [Word Category = Living Environment]	223.84	112.163	4.006	443.679	3.983	1	*
[Business source] & [Word Category = Transport]	40.105	112.163	179.731	259.942	0.128	1	0.721

Note
Many *p* values were too low to fit in this table. Therefore, statistically significant *p* values as smaller than 0.05 (two-tailed) are indicated by an asterisk.

ethics and values, as there are statistically significant relations identified between the business sources of information or SIA and the three sustainability terminology categories of behaviour, ethics and sustainable living environment. Second, there is no significant relation detected between Chinese business source of information and the word category of transportation and green travel options such as shared bike; green traffic; zero carbon transportation; green express; multimodal transport; low-carbon transportation; slow transportation system; smart express; maglev train (or *gaotie* in Chinese, high-speed railway); carbon-free traffic; and smart traffic. Similar patterns were found between the sources of information of official reports, government and politics and legal sources of information and the two key dimensions of the Chinese sustainable living discourse, i.e. environmentally responsible social behaviour and green social ethics and values. The similarities thus identified suggest strong influence from governmental and official sources of information on Chinese business sectors.

Interaction between Sustainability Word Categories (SWC) and Year of Publication (YOP)

The section explores the distribution of different word categories or discourse dimensions of sustainable living in China between 2000 and 2018. The corpus analyses help reveal the social patterns which underlie the introduction and local adaption of sustainability principles and values over the last two decades.

Table 8.6 shows that publications on *environmentally responsible behaviour* ranging from domestic waste classification and recycling, collective dinning to household energy consumption began to see significant growth as early as 2006. This suggests that *environmentally responsible behaviour* represents one of the first and key dimensions of the sustainable living discourse in China. This corpus finding implies that the SIAs or main sources of information have been deliberately and actively engaging with the public from the start of the green social reform movements. At the governmental level, the fourth five-year plan for public law education and promotion started to engage the public in the development of green communities, green schools and green families as early as 2001. From 2006, a number of environmental regulations, policies and pollution monitoring, and management practices provided further incentives to the public participation in the growing environmental debates. These include the publication of the regulations for the public participation in environmental impact assessment and environmental information disclosure and daily air quality monitoring reports for all prefecture-level cities in the country.

Table 8.6 Interaction between SWC and YOP: SWC=Behaviour

Word category and years	B	Std. error	95% Wald confidence interval		Hypothesis test		
			Lower	Upper	Wald chi-square	df	Sig.
[Responsible Behaviour] & [Year=2018]	575.000	164.86	251.864	898.136	12.164	1	*
[Responsible Behaviour] & [Year=2017]	1059.286	164.86	736.150	1382.422	41.281	1	*
[Responsible Behaviour] & [Year=2016]	881.571	164.86	558.436	1204.70	28.592	1	*
[Responsible Behaviour] & [Year=2015]	894.000	164.86	570.864	1217.13	29.404	1	*
[Responsible Behaviour] & [Year=2014]	640.571	164.86	317.436	963.707	15.096	1	*
[Responsible Behaviour] & [Year=2013]	575.000	164.86	251.864	898.136	12.164	1	*
[Responsible Behaviour] & [Year=2012]	669.857	164.86	346.721	992.993	16.508	1	*
[Responsible Behaviour] & [Year=2011]	709.714	164.86	386.578	1032.85	18.531	1	*
[Responsible Behaviour] & [Year=2010]	421.286	164.86	98.150	744.422	6.529	1	*
[Responsible Behaviour] & [Year=2009]	313.571	164.86	-9.564	636.707	3.617	1	*
[Responsible Behaviour] & [Year=2008]	343.857	164.86	20.721	666.993	4.350	1	*
[Responsible Behaviour] & [Year=2007]	491.143	164.86	168.007	814.279	8.874	1	*
[Responsible Behaviour] & [Year=2006]	408.143	164.86	85.007	731.279	6.128	1	*
[Responsible Behaviour] & [Year=2005]	294.571	164.86	-28.564	617.707	3.192	1	0.074
[Responsible Behaviour] & [Year=2004]	135.857	164.86	-187.279	458.993	0.679	1	0.410
[Responsible Behaviour] & [Year=2003]	93.286	164.86	-229.850	416.422	0.320	1	0.572
[Responsible Behaviour] & [Year=2002]	110.571	164.86	-212.564	433.707	0.450	1	0.502
[Responsible Behaviour] & [Year=2001]	52.714	164.86	-270.422	375.850	0.102	1	0.749
[Responsible Behaviour] & [Year=2000]	29.143	164.86	-293.993	352.279	0.031	1	0.860

Note
Many p values were too low to fit in this table. Therefore, statistically significant p values as smaller than 0.05 (two-tailed) are indicated by an asterisk.

Table 8.7 shows that the word category of green ethics and social responsibilities entered into the Chinese sustainable living discourse at a much later stage compared with the first word category of environmentally responsible behaviour. Publications on green ethics and social responsibilities began to see important growth from 2012. This suggests that the social assimilation and establishment of environmental values and principles began to take root in the social development discourse in China after half a decade of active government-led education and promotion of environmentally responsible behaviour among the general public. In fact, the social awareness of environmental protection and its impact on public health had reached a record level in 2012 that within the four month period of July and October, three large collective environmental protects took place in the prosperous south-east coast city Ningbo; Hainan Island in South China Sea and the more remote and socio-economically disadvantaged city of Shi Fang of Sichuan province, in south-west China. Environmental responsibilities and rights became widely recognized and endorsed by the public.

Table 8.8 shows that compared with the previous two lexical categories, the sub-class of Chinese translated sustainability terminology which promotes the public participation in and contribution to the construction of sustainable, green living environments, both physically and conceptually only began to grow at a significant level from 2016 onwards. This dimension of the sustainable living discourse thus represents a new and emerging area which is very likely to see important growth in the coming years, as the Chinese government and business sectors invest more in the construction of sustainable housing and social facilitates such as community green space, ecological residence, renewable energy building, smart homes, vertical greening, as well as the development of green urban development policies and strategies.

Table 8.7 Interaction between SWC and YOP: SWC = Ethics and Social Responsibilities

Parameter	B	Error	95% confidence interval		Hypothesis test Wald		
			Lower	Upper	Wald chi-square	df	Sig.
[Word Category = Ethics] & [Year = 2018]	1073.714	164.8683	750.578	1396.850	42.413	1	*
[Word Category = Ethics] & [Year = 2017]	1409.714	164.8683	1086.578	1732.850	73.112	1	*
[Word Category = Ethics] & [Year = 2016]	744.571	164.8683	421.436	1067.707	20.396	1	*
[Word Category = Ethics] & [Year = 2015]	728.714	164.8683	405.578	1051.850	19.536	1	*
[Word Category = Ethics] & [Year = 2014]	455.857	164.8683	132.721	778.993	7.645	1	*
[Word Category = Ethics] & [Year = 2013]	421.714	164.8683	98.578	744.850	6.543	1	*
[Word Category = Ethics] & [Year = 2012]	340.000	164.8683	16.864	663.136	4.253	1	0.039
[Word Category = Ethics] & [Year = 2011]	318.571	164.8683	-4.564	641.707	3.734	1	0.053
[Word Category = Ethics] & [Year = 2010]	150.429	164.8683	-172.707	473.564	0.833	1	0.362
[Word Category = Ethics] & [Year = 2009]	104.286	164.8683	-218.850	427.422	0.400	1	0.527
[Word Category = Ethics] & [Year = 2008]	121.143	164.8683	-201.993	444.279	0.540	1	0.462
[Word Category = Ethics] & [Year = 2007]	141.000	164.8683	-182.136	464.136	0.731	1	0.392
[Word Category = Ethics] & [Year = 2006]	156.714	164.8683	-166.422	479.850	0.904	1	0.342
[Word Category = Ethics] & [Year = 2005]	128.714	164.8683	-194.422	451.850	0.610	1	0.435
[Word Category = Ethics] & [Year = 2004]	70.000	164.8683	-253.136	393.136	0.180	1	0.671
[Word Category = Ethics] & [Year = 2003]	44.000	164.8683	-279.136	367.136	0.071	1	0.790
[Word Category = Ethics] & [Year = 2002]	53.286	164.8683	-269.850	376.422	0.104	1	0.747
[Word Category = Ethics] & [Year = 2001]	36.000	164.8683	-287.136	359.136	0.048	1	0.827
[Word Category = Ethics] & [Year = 2000]	21.857	164.8683	-301.279	344.993	0.018	1	0.895

Note
Many values were too low to fit in this table. Therefore, statistically significant p values as smaller than 0.05 (two-tailed) are indicated by an asterisk.

Table 8.8 Interaction between SWC and YOP: SWC=Sustainable Living Environment

Years	B	Error	95% Wald confidence interval		Hypothesis test Wald		
			Lower	Upper	Square	df	Sig.
[Word Category=Sustainable Living Environment] & [2018]	231.571	164.868	−91.564	554.707	1.973	1	0.160
[Word Category=Sustainable Living Environment] & [2017]	468.143	164.8683	145.007	791.279	8.063	1	*
[Word Category=Sustainable Living Environment] & [2016]	353.000	164.8683	29.864	676.136	4.584	1	*
[Word Category=Sustainable Living Environment] & [2015]	209.429	164.8683	−113.707	532.564	1.614	1	0.204
[Word Category=Sustainable Living Environment] & [2014]	143.000	164.8683	−180.136	466.136	0.752	1	0.386
[Word Category=Sustainable Living Environment] & [2013]	170.143	164.8683	−152.993	493.279	1.065	1	0.302
[Word Category=Sustainable Living Environment] & [2012]	200.286	164.8683	−122.850	523.422	1.476	1	0.224
[Word Category=Sustainable Living Environment] & [2011]	224.429	164.8683	−98.707	547.564	1.853	1	0.173
[Word Category=Sustainable Living Environment] & [2010]	94.429	164.8683	−228.707	417.564	0.328	1	0.567
[Word Category=Sustainable Living Environment] & [2009]	35.000	164.8683	−288.136	358.136	0.045	1	0.832
[Word Category=Sustainable Living Environment] & [2008]	37.286	164.8683	−285.850	360.422	0.051	1	0.821
[Word Category=Sustainable Living Environment] & [2007]	71.571	164.8683	−251.564	394.707	0.188	1	0.664
[Word Category=Sustainable Living Environment] & [2006]	122.857	164.8683	−200.279	445.993	0.555	1	0.456
[Word Category=Sustainable Living Environment] & [2005]	100.857	164.8683	−222.279	423.993	0.374	1	0.541
[Word Category=Sustainable Living Environment] & [2004]	38.143	164.8683	−284.993	361.279	0.054	1	0.817
[Word Category=Sustainable Living Environment] & [2003]	35.143	164.8683	−287.993	358.279	0.045	1	0.831
[Word Category=Sustainable Living Environment] & [2002]	60.143	164.8683	−262.993	383.279	0.133	1	0.715
[Word Category=Sustainable Living Environment] & [2001]	18.571	164.8683	−304.564	341.707	0.013	1	0.910
[Word Category=Sustainable Living Environment] & [2000]	7.571	164.8683	−315.564	330.707	0.002	1	0.963

Note
Many values were too low to fit in this table. Therefore, statistically significant p values as smaller than 0.05 (two-tailed) are indicated by an asterisk.

9 Diffusion of sustainable living discourse in China and Japan

Having explicated the data collection process and the model design and aims above, this chapter now turns to the presentation and explanation of the results of the statistical tests performed on the overall model. The discussion is divided into three sections based on the three empirical models which inform the overall structural equation model constructed. The first section presents and discusses the findings concerning the influence from main sources of information on industrial end-users; the second section provides the results for and discusses the mediating effects of the media; while the third and final section explicates the findings on the Multi-Sectoral Interaction (MSI) among sources of information and the media. In studying the three proposed social mechanisms in our target countries, the current study develops and verifies advanced corpus analytical methods, with a view to providing insights and suggestions for evidence-based policy-making at national and international levels.

This section offers a data-driven empirical study of the translation, adaptation and diffusion of clean energy production and consumption discourses in the last twenty years in China and Japan. The translation and social dissemination of the principles and suggestions provided by organizations of global governance such as the UN in terms of achieving SDGs in national contexts requires not only effective MSI among social sectors, but also relies on the existence of an effective social transmission network able to link the main sources of information, such as government agencies, industrial and business sources, with the end-users of the information distributed, i.e. a wide range of industrial sectors. It employs quantitative corpus linguistic methods and political discourse analysis in order to identify and construct a formalized empirical model of the social dissemination and culturally adapted development of clean and renewable energy production and consumption discourses in China and Japan.

In doing so, it illustrates through structural equation modelling three important components of diffusion. First, it illustrates the pathways of social accountability attribution, which is proposed to describe the frequencies of occurrence or levels of importance given to industrial sectors in materials published by different sources of information when discussing clean and renewable energy production and consumption. Second, it assesses the role of the media as a social intervention able to be moderated in a way to alter the social accountability attribution pathways. Third, it demonstrates MSI among sources of information, i.e. governmental, business, industrial, official, legal, etc. to be an integral part of the social accountability attribution process. It is hypothesized that stronger MSI may foster better overall environmental performance to achieve UN SDGs. For this purpose, the MSI scores across the three topical areas of clean or renewable energy generation and consumption were computed. The resulting MSI composite scores were then compared against the global Environmental Performance Index (EPI) to verify the hypothesis of MSI as an important social mechanism for the adaptation, diffusion and uptake of SDGs championed by the UN.

Sources of information interpreting sustainability

This section examines the levels of direct effects from different sources of information in the enhancement of the visibility of different socio-industrial sectors. These involve three sets of data which are dependent, independent and mediating variables. The latter two are also known as exogenous variables in structural equation modelling or path analysis. We address three independent variables, which are Business, Top Industry and Government/Political sources, and two mediating variables, newspapers and magazines/journals. The dependent variables are the eighteen industrial sectors provided in the previous section. This classification framework for the sources of information and industrial sectors aligns with the structure of the Factiva database. The following section examines the social accountability attribution process that underscores the diffusion of renewable energy discourses related to lifestyle/behavioural changes and societal/national visions of change. The corpus analysis drew upon the word lists compiled for China and Japan, provided in the previous section (see also Appendices 1 and 2).

Table 9.1 shows the statistically significant regression weights identified in the corpus analysis of the occurrence of industrial sectors among business sources. In the formalized analysis of the development of renewable and clean energy discourses, the predictive relationship between the independent variables and the dependent variable can be measured by the regression weight or coefficient. In structural equation modelling, unstandardized regression weights indicate the amount of variance in the dependent variable per single unit change in the predictor variable. Large positive unstandardized regression weights are indicative of the strong impact of the independent variable on the dependent variable. For example, in Table 9.1, the large direct impact of business sources on the agriculture sector in China is indicated by the large unstandardized regression coefficient 3.107. By contract, the limited impact from business sources on the agriculture sector in Japan is reflected in the small regression coefficient of −0.962. Their associated critical ratios (C.R. in the table) are 3.107 and −0.962. The threshold value of the critical ratio is 1.965, meaning that only when the absolute value of the critical ratio is 1.965 or above, or −1.965 or less, is it a statistically significant relationship detected between the independent and the dependent variables. Based on the critical ratios provided above, it is inferred that while business sources in China make a statistically significant contribution to the visibility of the agriculture sector in public discussion and reporting of lifestyle and behavioural change as part of the clean/renewable energy consumption discourse, this is not the case in Japan because the critical ratio does not exceed the threshold.

Similar analyses were conducted across the eighteen industrial sectors as shown in Table 9.1. Three important patterns regarding the differences and similarities between the two countries begin to emerge. An *asymmetrical* pattern is found when a statistically significant relationship is only detected in one country, as in the case of the Automotive, Financial Services and Technology sectors in business sources. This is statistically significant in Japan, but not in China. A *contrastive* pattern is evident when the regression coefficients have positive versus negative values: a positive value indicates the enhanced visibility of an industrial sector in business source materials; whereas a negative value suggests that an industrial sector is under-reported in business source materials. Contrastive patterns between the two countries can be identified in sectors such as Alternative Fuels, Business and Consumer Services, Industrial Goods and Utilities: while Japanese business sources have given these sectors important visibility, these sectors are largely under-reported in Chinese business sources. A *complementary* pattern is established when business sources in the two countries are found to give similar importance, or the lack of it, to an industrial sector in their publications. This is the case of Consumer Goods, where the regression coefficients are both negative, and the case of Transport/Logistics, where the regression coefficients are both positive scores.

Table 9.2 shows the direct effects from government and political sources on the visibility of different industrial sectors in the Factiva database. The patterns to emerge from a comparison of the two countries

Table 9.1 Direct effects from business sources on industrial sectors

Dependent variable	Country	Independent variables	Estimate	S.E.	C.R.	P	Patterns
Agriculture	CHN	Business sources	0.239	0.077	3.107	*	Asymmetrical
	JPN	Business sources	-0.061	0.064	-0.962	0.336	
Alternative Fuels	CHN	Business sources	-0.136	0.013	-10.402	*	Contrastive
	JPN	Business sources	0.353	0.145	2.43	*	
Automotive	CHN	Business sources	-0.002	0.058	-0.026	0.979	Asymmetrical
	JPN	Business sources	0.407	0.122	3.338	*	
Business and Consumer Services	CHN	Business sources	-0.289	0.071	-4.1	*	Contrastive
	JPN	Business sources	0.811	0.172	4.722	*	
Consumer Goods	CHN	Business sources	-0.057	0.019	-3.021	*	Complementary
	JPN	Business sources	-0.251	0.061	-4.104	*	
Electric Power Generation	CHN	Business sources	-0.722	0.301	-2.401	*	Contrastive
	JPN	Business sources	0.191	0.298	0.64	0.522	
Financial Services	CHN	Business sources	0.256	0.233	1.098	0.272	Asymmetrical
	JPN	Business sources	0.485	0.102	4.744	*	
Industrial Goods	CHN	Business sources	-0.305	0.097	-3.163	*	Contrastive
	JPN	Business sources	2.032	0.491	4.141	*	
Leisure and Hospitality	CHN	Business sources	-0.046	0.019	-2.429	*	Contrastive
	JPN	Business sources	0.132	0.036	3.657	*	
Media Entertainment	CHN	Business sources	-0.021	0.006	-3.517	*	Asymmetrical
	JPN	Business sources	0.008	0.023	0.323	0.747	
Real Estate Construction	CHN	Business sources	-0.283	0.109	-2.603	*	Contrastive
	JPN	Business sources	0.619	0.17	3.637	*	
Retail Wholesale	CHN	Business sources	-0.026	0.005	-4.971	*	Asymmetrical
	JPN	Business sources	0.125	0.101	1.236	0.216	
Technology	CHN	Business sources	0.167	0.11	1.51	0.131	Asymmetrical
	JPN	Business sources	1.151	0.413	2.784	*	
Telecommunication	CHN	Business sources	-0.013	0.009	-1.521	0.128	Asymmetrical
	JPN	Business sources	-0.505	0.098	-5.167	*	
Transport and Logistics	CHN	Business sources	0.092	0.022	4.136	*	Complementary
	JPN	Business sources	0.142	0.049	2.904	*	
Utilities	CHN	Business sources	-1.406	0.492	-2.858	*	Contrastive
	JPN	Business sources	4.928	1.148	4.292	*	

Note

Some values were too low to fit in this table. Therefore, statistically significant p values as smaller than 0.05 (two-tailed) are indicated by an asterisk

Country	Dependent variable	Independent variables	Estimate	S.E.	C.R.	P	Pattern
CHN	Agriculture	Government and Politics	-0.194	0.075	-2.572	*	Asymmetrical
JPN		Government and Politics	0.16	0.227	0.706	0.48	Asymmetrical
CHN	Alternative Fuels	Government and Politics	0.144	0.013	11.273	*	Asymmetrical
JPN		Government and Politics	-0.124	0.516	-0.24	0.81	Asymmetrical
CHN	Automotive	Government and Politics	0.07	0.057	1.233	0.217	Asymmetrical
JPN		Government and Politics	-1.185	0.434	-2.729	*	Asymmetrical
CHN	Business and Consumer Services	Government and Politics	0.355	0.069	5.152	*	Asymmetrical
JPN		Government and Politics	-0.512	0.612	-0.837	0.403	Asymmetrical
CHN	Consumer Goods	Government and Politics	0.067	0.018	3.643	*	Asymmetrical
JPN		Government and Politics	0.394	0.218	1.811	0.07	Asymmetrical
CHN	Electric Power Generation	Government and Politics	1.025	0.294	3.486	*	Asymmetrical
JPN		Government and Politics	2.002	1.06	1.888	0.059	Asymmetrical
CHN	Financial Services	Government and Politics	-0.053	0.228	-0.232	0.817	Asymmetrical
JPN		Government and Politics	1.149	0.364	3.155	0.002	Asymmetrical
CHN	Healthcare and Life Science	Government and Politics	0	0.051	-0.003	0.998	Asymmetrical
JPN		Government and Politics	0.273	0.054	5.028	*	Asymmetrical
CHN	Industrial Goods	Government and Politics	0.378	0.094	4.004	*	Asymmetrical
JPN		Government and Politics	1.555	1.747	0.89	0.373	Asymmetrical
CHN	Leisure and Hospitality	Government and Politics	0.062	0.018	3.334	*	Asymmetrical
JPN		Government and Politics	0.23	0.129	1.787	0.074	Asymmetrical
CHN	Media and Entertainment	Government and Politics	0.019	0.006	3.37	*	Asymmetrical
JPN		Government and Politics	0.105	0.083	1.259	0.208	Asymmetrical
CHN	Nuclear Fuel	Government and Politics	-0.002	0.004	-0.645	0.519	Asymmetrical
JPN		Government and Politics	-0.185	0.05	-3.705	*	Asymmetrical
CHN	Real Estate and Construction	Government and Politics	0.509	0.106	4.791	*	Contrastive
JPN		Government and Politics	-1.202	0.606	-1.985	0.047	Asymmetrical
CHN	Retail Wholesale	Government and Politics	0.021	0.005	4.229	*	Asymmetrical
JPN		Government and Politics	-0.43	0.359	-1.2	0.23	Asymmetrical
CHN	Telecommunication	Government and Politics	0.018	0.008	2.116	0.034	Asymmetrical
JPN		Government and Politics	-0.036	0.348	-0.104	0.917	Asymmetrical
CHN	Transport and Logistics	Government and Politics	-0.09	0.022	-4.109	*	Asymmetrical
JPN		Government and Politics	0.09	0.174	0.52	0.603	Asymmetrical
CHN	Utilities	Government and Politics	1.843	0.481	3.83	*	Asymmetrical
JPN		Government and Politics	4.828	4.088	1.181	0.238	Asymmetrical

Note
Some values were too low to fit in this table. Therefore, statistically significant p values as smaller than 0.05 (two-tailed) are indicated by an asterisk.

exhibit important differences from those identified in Table 9.1. Specifi-cally, more asymmetrical patterns are evident between the two countries which suggest very different governmental and political focuses and approaches to the promotion of the lifestyle/behavioural and societal change in the context of transitioning to clean/renewable energy systems among industrial sectors. For instance, the following industrial sectors were mentioned very frequently in the Chinese government and political sources, but were not a statistically significant presence in Japanese gov-ernmental and political sources: Alternative Fuels; Business & Consumer Services; Consumer Goods; Electric Power Generation; Industrial Goods; Leisure and Hospitality; Media and Entertainment; Real Estate and Con-struction; Retail and Wholesale; Telecommunication and Utilities.

The industrial sectors with a strong presence among Japanese govern-ment and political sources are Healthcare and Life Science, and Financial Services. Some industrial sectors were under-represented in Japanese political and governmental sources as indicated by the larger negative regression coefficients. These were Automotive, Nuclear fuel as well as Real Estate and Construction. The asymmetrical patterns detected between the two countries suggest that, while the Chinese government and political sources served to establish a wider range of association between lifestyle/behavioural and societal change brought about by clean/renewable energy, there is focus on areas such as Healthcare and Life Science and Financial Services, among the Japanese governmental and political sources, possibly because substantial innovation in these areas could bring more substantial change to people's everyday lives particular with respect to the challenges on the healthcare provision in Japan owing to the onset of the hyper-aged society.

Table 9.3 shows the comparison between China and Japan in terms of the visibility of different industrial sectors in information published by the top industrial sources of the two countries. Similar to the corpus findings presented in Table 9.2, asymmetrical patterns remain the key feature dis-tinguishing the two countries. The two industrial sectors which were most mentioned in Chinese top industrial sources when discussing lifestyle/behavioural and societal changes were Agriculture and Healthcare/Life Science. By contrast, the industrial sector which gained a strong presence in Japanese top industrial sources was Consumer Goods. A number of complementary patterns emerged from the corpus analysis as well, despite the important differences detected between the two countries. For example, Industrial Goods and Technology were the two sectors which were largely under-reported among top industrial sources of both countries. On the other hand, the Telecommunication sector was heavily reported among top industrial sources in both countries when discussing the relationship of this

Table 9.3 Direct effects from top industry sources on industrial sectors

Country	Dependent variable	Independent variables	Estimate	S.E.	C.R.	P	Pattern
CHN	Agriculture	Top Industry Sources	0.749	0.35	2.137	0.033	Asymmetrical
JPN		Top Industry Sources	0.021	0.145	0.147	0.884	
CHN	Alternative Fuels	Top Industry Sources	0.112	0.059	1.888	0.059	Asymmetrical
JPN		Top Industry Sources	-1.727	0.33	-5.231	*	
CHN	Consumer Goods	Top Industry Sources	0.135	0.086	1.581	0.114	Asymmetrical
JPN		Top Industry Sources	0.63	0.139	4.524	*	
CHN	Financial Services	Top Industry Sources	-1.989	1.061	-1.874	0.061	Asymmetrical
JPN		Top Industry Sources	-0.874	0.233	-3.756	*	
CHN	Healthcare and Life Science	Top Industry Sources	0.543	0.235	2.306	0.021	Asymmetrical
JPN		Top Industry Sources	-0.009	0.035	-0.247	0.805	
CHN	Industrial Goods	Top Industry Sources	-0.999	0.439	-2.277	0.023	Complementary
JPN		Top Industry Sources	-4.649	1.117	-4.164	*	
CHN	Retail and Wholesale	Top Industry Sources	0.027	0.023	1.152	0.249	Asymmetrical
JPN		Top Industry Sources	-0.785	0.229	-3.426	*	
CHN	Technology	Top Industry Sources	-1.566	0.501	-3.123	0.002	Complementary
JPN		Top Industry Sources	-3.149	0.941	-3.347	*	
CHN	Telecommunication	Top Industry Sources	0.148	0.039	3.81	0.036	Complementary
JPN		Top Industry Sources	0.468	0.223	2.101	*	
CHN	Transport and Logistics	Top Industry Sources	-0.363	0.102	-3.572	*	Asymmetrical
JPN		Top Industry Sources	0.06	0.111	0.543	0.587	
CHN	Utilities	Top Industry Sources	-3.187	2.238	-1.424	0.154	Asymmetrical
JPN		Top Industry Sources	-9.916	2.613	-3.794	*	

Note
Some values were too low to fit in this table. Therefore, statistically significant *p* values as smaller than 0.05 (two-tailed) are indicated by an asterisk.

sector with people's everyday lives amid the growing discourse of 'green' and 'sustainable' ethics in lifestyle and consumption habits, analogous to the cultivation and dissemination of environmental norms.

The corpus analysis in this section constructed models of multilevel governance for Renewable Energy Production and Consumption and Social Innovation in China and Japan. Joyeeta Gupta and Mans Nilsson (Gupta and Nilsson 2017: 278) propose the new governance model and approach of '*multilevel governance*' which means that the 'central state does not monopolise action, but interacts in many different ways with actors at subnational, supranational and international levels' (p. 278). Hooghe and Marks (2003: 235) observe that '*governance diffusion and desperation* allows for the internalisation of externalities, gives space for heterogeneity and preferences, and allows for multiple arenas of innovation and experimentation'. The corpus analysis provides solid empirical analyses which assess and compare the direct effects from different social actors that form the emerging multilevel governance for renewable energy production, consumption and related social innovation in China and Japan. These entail the comparison of the influence from governmental, business, industrial, legal and research agencies on the adaption, diffusion and sectorally motivated integration of clean energy related SDGs in China and Japan. Specifically, our study tested the underlying hypothesis that, in the transmission and adaptation of global SDGs in different national contexts, three large groups of social actors encompassing sources of information, mediating actors and socio-industrial end-users form, shape and contribute to the complex, latent networks of social engagement. It does so in order to illuminate how the distribution within these networks largely determines the level and breadth of the diffusion of global SDGs and their associated environmentalist norms, knowledge of which is essential for informing policy-making at national and international levels.

The role of the mass media

We will elaborate on the process of constructing empirical analytical instruments to assess, compare and illustrate the mediating effect of the media such as newspapers, magazines and journals on the diffusion and adaptive integration of SDGs related to clean energy discourse in China and Japan. Gupta and Mason (2014) offers a critical assessment of whether transparency is a broadly transformative force in global environmental governance or plays a more limited role. Their case studies which focus on issue areas including climate change, biodiversity, biotechnology, natural resource exploitation and chemicals, demonstrate that although transparency is ubiquitous, its effects are limited and often specific to particular contexts. The empirical study of the media as a major transparency source in China and Japan challenges the findings offered in Gupta and Mason (2014). Different from the qualitative case studies of Gupta and Mason, our study is essentially quantitative and data-driven which is based on the statistical analyses of large amounts of original Chinese and Japanese materials from a variety of sources, e.g. governmental, industrial, business, legal and research institutions. Our findings suggest that while systematic alignment between main social agencies of environmental governance, e.g. governmental, large business and top industrial institutions and the media – this is termed as the limited instrumental role of transparency in Gupta and Mason (2014) – important differences do exist between them at both subnational and supranational levels.

We analyse and measure such similarities and divergences by specifying the direct effects of the main social agencies of environmental governance on industrial sectors and their indirect effects from the media when entering the media as a mediating variable into the statistically derived social diffusion model. We found that while in some cases the direct effects from main social agencies are in the same direction as the indirect effects from the media in the promotion of social innovation around environmental governance, the indirect effects from the media can be significantly different posing real challenges to the institutional agencies of environmental governance and this complex and growing social phenomenon can be observed in the patterns uncovered in longitudinal Chinese and Japanese resources related to the social diffusion and integration of SDGs of clean energy consumption, production, related social innovation and lifestyle and behavioural transition.

The second of the three social mechanisms proposed in this book which underlines the transmission of clean/renewable energy consumption discourse is the social mediation carried out by the mass media. This section examines the indirect or mediating effects of the media on the relationship between sources of information and different socio-industrial end-users, illustrating the function of the media as a social intervention instrument. Specifically, this section examines the indirect effects of newspapers and magazines/journals on the social visibility given to or social engagement with industrial sectors by three large sources of information, i.e. top industry sources, government/political sources and business sources. The cross-national analysis of the mediating social function of the media aims to demonstrate the contrasts in the social function of the media between the two countries.

Table 9.4 shows a comparison of the indirect effects from the media on the relationships between top industry sources and a range of industrial sectors in China and Japan. The indirect effect values shown in the Top

Table 9.4 Indirect effects of the media on top industrial sources and industrial sector relationship

Dependent variable	Direct effects Top Industry Sources CHN	Indirect effect Top Industry Sources CHN	Direct effects Top Industry Sources JPN	Indirect effect Top Industry Sources JPN
Agriculture	0.749	0.395	0.021	0.249
Alternative Fuels	0.112	-0.179	-1.727	0.633
Automotive	0.239	-0.025	-0.324	0.735
Business and Consumer Services	-0.363	-0.562	-0.392	-0.212
Consumer Goods	0.315	-0.138	0.63	0.451
Electric Power Generation	0.001	-1.213	0.127	1.73
Financial Services	-1.989	-0.294	-0.874	-0.223
Healthcare Life Science	0.543	0.03	-0.009	-0.035
Industrial Goods	-0.999	-0.87	-4.649	0.134
Leisure Hospitality	0.043	-0.038	-0.072	-0.096
Media Entertainment	0.052	-0.026	0.005	0.021
Nuclear Fuel	-0.001	0.006	0.045	0.055
Real Estate Construction	0.163	-0.451	0.598	0.163
Retail Wholesale	0.027	-0.045	-0.785	0.486
Technology	-1.566	-0.146	-3.149	1.024
Telecommunication	0.148	0.01	0.468	0.765
Transport Logistics	-0.363	-0.005	0.06	-0.042
Utilities	-3.187	-3.083	-9.916	-0.665

Industry Sources columns represent the combination of the mediating effects from both newspapers and magazines/journals. These were calculated based on the combined unstandardized regression coefficients in the structural equation modelling. The correlation coefficient of the two sets of indirect effects from the media in China and Japan is 0.220. This suggests that there is limited similarity in the social intervention function of the media in both countries. Positive indirect effects as opposed to negative direct effects with the Japanese data point to how, in most cases, when the Japanese mass media do not align with top industry sources, the media play an enhancing role by raising the visibility of industrial sectors in public reports, as in cases where these sectors do not enjoy a strong presence or are significantly under-represented in Japanese top industry sources on lifestyle/behaviour and societal change in the context of the transition to clean/renewable energy systems. These sectors include Alternative Fuels, Automotive, Retail/Wholesale and Technology in the Japanese data set. The Chinese comparative data set presents a very different picture, as the positive direct effects from top industry sources tend to co-align with the negative indirect effects from the media. This means that, while a range of industrial sectors have been given important visibility in publications from Chinese top industry sources, these sectors were under-reported in the Chinese media. These sectors are Alternative Fuels, Automotive, Consumer Goods, Electric Generation, Leisure and Hospitality, Media and Entertainment, Real Estate and Construction and Retail/Wholesale.

Table 9.5 shows the result of Spearman's correlation test of the strength of the correlation between the direct and indirect effects of top industry sources on industrial sectors in China. The correlation coefficient is 0.600 which is statistically significant at the 0.01 level (two-tailed). This result highlights the strong correlation between the top industry sources in China and the mass media regarding discourses on the change in people's lifestyles and habits as well as societal/national visions of change in the context of transitioning to clean/renewable energy systems. This statistically significant alignment also indicates the Chinese media's lack of independence from top industry, despite the detected differences in the values of direct effects and indirect effects from the media.

Table 9.6 shows the result of Spearman's test of the strength of correlation between direct effects from the Japanese top industrial sources and the indirect effects from the Japanese mass media. The correlation coefficient is 0.316. This is not statistically significant at the 0.01 level (two-tailed). Therefore, the result suggests that the direct effects and indirect effects are independent of each other without strong correlation between them. Thus, in contrast to China, the Japanese mass media is independent of the reporting

Table 9.5 Spearman's test of the correlation between Chinese top industry sources and the media

			Direct	Indirect
Spearman's rho	Direct	Correlation coefficient	1.000	0.600
		Sig. (two-tailed)		0.008
		N of valid cases	18	18
	Indirect	Correlation coefficient	0.600	1.000
		Sig. (two-tailed)	0.008	
		N of valid cases	18	18

Table 9.6 Spearman's test of the correlation between Japanese top industry sources and the media

			Direct	Indirect
Spearman's rho	Direct	Correlation coefficient	1.000	0.251
		Sig. (two-tailed)		0.316
		N of valid cases	18	18
	Indirect	Correlation coefficient	0.251	1.000
		Sig. (two-tailed)	0.316	
		N of valid cases	18	18

and publications of the top industry sources regarding industrial contribution to and engagement with people's lifestyle change through innovation in clean/renewable energy production and consumption.

Table 9.7 shows the Spearman's test of the strength of correlation between direct and indirect effects of the government/political sources in China. The correlation coefficient is -0.0688, which is statistically significant at the 0.01 level (two-tailed). This suggests that the reporting of the Chinese media on clean/renewable energy and people's lifestyle change is significantly different from publications on similar issues by government/political sources. The independence of the Chinese mass media from government/political sources on the reporting of this particular issue appears to be verified by the corpus data.

Table 9.8 shows the result of the correlation test with the direct and indirect effects of Japanese government/political sources of information and the Japanese mass media. There was very limited correlation between the direct and indirect effects as the correlation coefficient was 0.102, which is not statistically significant at the 0.01 level (two-tailed). This result again testifies to the relative independence of the Japanese mass media from Japanese government/political sources of information in the reporting of sectoral

Table 9.7 Spearman's test of correlation between Chinese government and political sources and the media

			Direct	Indirect
Spearman's rho	Direct	Correlation coefficient	1.000	−0.688
		Sig. (two-tailed)		0.002
		N of valid cases	18	18
	Indirect	Correlation coefficient	−0.688	1.000
		Sig. (two-tailed)	0.002	
		N of valid cases	18	18

Table 9.8 Spearman's test of correlation between Japanese government and political sources and the media

			Direct	Indirect
Spearman's rho	Direct	Correlation coefficient	1.000	−0.102
		Sig. (two-tailed)		0.687
		N of valid cases	18	18
	Indirect	Correlation coefficient	−0.102	1.000
		Sig. (two-tailed)	0.687	
		N of valid cases	18	18

contribution to and involvement in people's changing lifestyle and behaviours with the transmission and translation of the clean/renewable energy discourse as a new and integral part of our contemporary life.

Table 9.9 shows the correlation test of direct and indirect effects from Chinese business sources and the Chinese mass media. The correlation coefficient is −0.657 which is statistically significant at the two-tailed 0.01 level. This is similar to the pattern identified in Table 9.7 in which the Chinese government/political sources had a strong negative correlation with the Chinese mass media. This result points to the fact that the Chinese media takes a very different approach from Chinese business sources in the reporting of clean/renewable energy consumption in China.

Table 9.10 shows the correlation test result of the direct and indirect effects from Japanese business sources and the Japanese mass media. The correlation coefficient is −0.628 which is statistically significant at the two-tailed 0.01 level. This indicates that the Japanese media is significantly different from Japanese business sources in reporting on the topic of clean/renewable energy and people's lifestyle change as related to different industrial sectors in the country. We see here that, while the Japanese mass media exhibits clear independence from Japanese top industrial and

Table 9.9 Spearman's test of correlation between Chinese business sources and the media

			Direct	Indirect
Spearman's rho	Direct	Correlation coefficient	1.000	−0.657
		Sig. (two-tailed)		0.003
		N of valid cases	18	18
	Indirect	Correlation coefficient	−0.657	1.000
		Sig. (two-tailed)	0.003	
		N of valid cases	18	18

Table 9.10 Spearman's test of correlation between Japanese business sources and the media

			Direct	Indirect
Spearman's rho	Direct	Correlation coefficient	1.000	−0.628
		Sig. (two-tailed)		0.005
		N of valid cases	18	18
	Indirect	Correlation coefficient	−0.628	1.000
		Sig. (two-tailed)	0.005	
		N of valid cases	18	18

government/political sources, it has taken a very different approach from business sources. The large negative correlation score extracted from the Japanese data is comparable to the one identified in the Chinese data.

As stated previously, the corpus analysis built empirical analytical instruments to assess, compare and illustrate the mediating effect of the media on the diffusion and integration of SDGs related to clean and renewable energies in China and Japan. From this, we found that while in some cases the direct effects from main social agencies are in the same direction of the indirect effects from the media in the promotion of social innovation around environmental governance, the indirect effects from the media can be significantly different. This poses real challenges to the institutional agencies of environmental governance and this complex and growing social phenomenon can be observed in the patterns uncovered in longitudinal Chinese and Japanese resources related to the social diffusion and integration of SDGs of clean energy consumption, production, related social, industrial innovation and lifestyle and behavioural transition. Although this is not necessarily at odds with other assessments on the role of systematic industrial alignment which suggest it is limited at best (e.g. Gupta and Mason 2014) as a transformatory force, our findings suggest the existence of important differences at both subnational and supranational levels which also play a facilitatory or hindering role in the communication of environmental ethics and practices. In other words, by examining what is both communicated and what is not communicated across different industrial sectors, we are able to examine the ways in which any transformation, limited or otherwise, is facilitated or hindered within different national polities.

Interaction between sustainability interpreting agents and the mass media

This section will demonstrate that multi-sectoral interaction can be a powerful intervention mechanism for effective policy-making in tackling environmental risks management issues requiring important cross-sectoral collaboration. The development of the empirical analytical instrument of multi-sectoral interaction helps us to close the gaps in the intra-sectoral understanding and action taken around environmental health communication and management among sectoral stakeholders to build much-needed multi-sectoral and cross-national cooperation. In addition, multi-sectoral interaction also affords us a tool to understand another dimension of the communication of the transition to a clean/renewable energy system, namely cross-sectoral conformity and divergence over environmental issues that are widely considered to require significant collaboration to suitably address.

It is hypothesized that the communication of lifestyle/behavioural changes in the context of transitioning to clean/renewable energy in order to meet the targets of the SDGs established by the UN and its affiliates depends on strong multi-sectoral interaction among the main information sources of a polity including the media to enhance the country's environmental performance as measured by the EPI. Based on this, the higher the multi-sectoral interaction among the various information sources, the better the overall environmental performance of that country. The MSI instrument serves as an indicator of the effectiveness of cross-sectoral environmental communication which underscores the environmental performance of the two countries under comparison. This section will test whether the hypothesized multi-sectoral interaction mechanism holds true for China and Japan, which represent different socio-economic and political systems as well as environmental cultures.

The multi-sectoral interaction score is developed as an empirical instrument, enabling us to make multi-sectoral and cross-country comparisons. The multi-sectoral interaction matrix provides the breakdown of the correlation scores for each pair of the five large environmental communication agencies in each country. For example, between governmental sources and top industry sources, or business sources and newspapers, or magazines and newspapers, etc. The correlation scores for each sectoral pair indicate the strength of association between the two sectors selected. These correlation scores by sector pairs reveal the level of MSI in China and Japan. Tables 9.11 and 9.12 show the matrices of correlation scores among different information sources in the two countries: top industrial sources, government/political sources and business sources and the mass media, i.e. newspapers and magazines/journals. The correlation coefficient measures the strength of association between two variables, or the two information sources.

The coefficient scores range between negative one and positive one. Zero indicates no relation between the two variables. Within the positive spectrum of correlation, the larger the correlation coefficient, the stronger the relation between the two variables, with positive one indicating two identical variables. For example, the first column of Table 9.11 shows that, in China, newspapers are strongly correlated with government/political sources (0.748), business sources (0.773) and magazines/journals (0.747), but only have a moderate correlation with top industry sources (0.451). The last row of the table displays the sum of the correlation scores by source of information. When there is no relation between any pair of sectors, then the sum of the correlation coefficients is zero. The correlation score sums range between 5 and −5.

In order to compare the two countries, the composite scores for China and Japan were computed through the sum of inter-sectoral correlation scores. The resulting composite scores can be used to compare the level of multi-sectoral interaction between the two countries (Table 9.13). The correlation composite scores are then compared with the widely used EPI, which provides the ranking of world countries based on their national performance in achieving two objectives, i.e. protection of human health and maintenance of the country's ecosystems (see Chapter 4). The availability of the index has enabled evidence-based environmental policy-making at national and international levels (Hsu *et al.* 2016). Table 9.13 shows the comparison between EPI scores and the multi-sectoral interaction composite scores for China and Japan. The index provides an empirical analytical instrument which ranks the countries in the world on nine priority environmental issues including air quality, forests, fisheries, climate and energy, among others. The chief objective of the EPI is to facilitate the transition from rhetorical environmental debates to the empirical study of environmental accountability among stakeholders and the outcomes in terms of a country's overall performance. Since its first pilot edition published in 2002, the EPI has served as an international reference

Table 9.11 Correlation matrix for Chinese sources of information

Sources	Correlation between vectors of values				
	Newspapers	*Top Industries*	*Government/ Politics*	*Business Sources*	*Magazine and Journals*
Newspapers	1.000	0.451	0.748	0.773	0.747
Top Industry Sources	0.451	1.000	0.169	0.252	0.456
Government and Politics	0.748	0.169	1.000	0.980	0.545
Business Sources	0.773	0.252	0.980	1.000	0.572
Magazine and Journals	0.747	0.456	0.545	0.572	1.000
Correlation composite score	3.719	2.327	3.442	3.578	3.320

Table 9.12 Correlation matrix for Japanese sources of information

Sources	Correlation between vectors of values				
	Newspapers	Top Industries	Government/ Politics	Business Sources	Magazine and Journals
Newspapers	1.000	0.922	0.808	0.978	0.902
Top Industry Sources	0.922	1.000	0.806	0.858	0.930
Government and Politics	0.808	0.806	1.000	0.817	0.873
Business Sources	0.978	0.858	0.817	1.000	0.872
Magazine and Journals	0.902	0.930	0.873	0.872	1.000
Correlation composite score	4.612	4.516	4.305	4.526	4.578

Table 9.13 Comparison between correlation composite scores with EPI scores

	Correlation composite scores	EPI scores
CHN	16.386	43 (ranked 118 globally on the 2014 EPI)
JPN	22.537	72.35 (ranked 26 globally on the 2014 EPI)

standard for comparing country performance on international policies, including the UN SDGs to effectively combat environmental degradation and climate change (Emerson *et al.* 2010). The current study uses the latest 2016 edition of the national EPI. A chi-square test was used to compare the two sets of ranking scores. If the hypothesis proposed holds true, i.e. strong correlation exists between the multi-sectoral interaction scores and the EPI scores which measure multi-sectoral interaction among information sources in each country and the country's environmental performance, respectively a non-significant chi-square score must be detected as the test cannot reject the null hypothesis, that is, the two ranking schemes are largely similar. If important differences emerge from comparing the two ranking instruments, then the original hypothesis may require rejecting or reformulating in terms of the relevance of the multi-sectoral interaction to national environmental performance. With a chi-square statistic of 0.1628 and a *p*-value of 0.686625, the results are not significant at $p < 0.05$. In other words, the level of multi-sectoral interaction aligns closely with a country's EPI score and so the multi-sectoral interaction can thus be used as an indicator of a country's overall environmental performance.

Multi-sectoral interaction, cooperation and partnerships development at subnational levels is an under-explored area of study in environmental governance, partly due to the lack of effective analytical models or solid social instruments to gauge and compare the levels of interaction among main institutional agencies of environmental governance. Our study developed and tested the first set of analytical tools to enable cross-national comparative studies of the social diffusion and integration of SDGs related to clean energy consumption and production, social and industrial innovation and lifestyle transition towards sustainable life in China and Japan. The corpus analysis in this section demonstrated that multi-sectoral interaction can be a powerful intervention mechanism for effective policy-making in tackling environmental risks management issues which require important cross-sectoral collaboration. The development of the empirical analytical instrument of multi-sectoral interaction can help close gaps in the intra-sectoral understanding and action taking around environmental communication and management among sectoral stakeholders to build much-needed multi-sectoral and cross-national cooperation. The differences between the two countries in terms of multi-sectoral interaction around the social diffusion, culture-specific interpretation and local integration of the principled environmental governance requirements were compared with the widely endorsed global EPI. The strong alignment between our findings and the EPI scores verified the theoretical hypothesis that stronger multi-sectoral interaction at the national level can effectively enhance the overall environmental performance of a country.

Conclusion

How to build effective global governance frameworks to stimulate sectoral, subnational and supranational cooperation around the UN SDGs poses both challenges and opportunities for national and international policymakers. This book pioneers the development of empirical political instruments for the integration of adaptive SDGs not only in East Asia but also at international level. The three analytical instruments developed can be used as social intervention tools in evidence-based policy-making to measure, monitor and intervene in the development of new social growth models, with a view to facilitating and enhancing the social diffusion of global SDGs. We construct models of multilevel governance for renewable energy production, consumption and social innovation in China and Japan. Joyeeta Gupta and Mans Nilsson (Kanie and Biermann 2017: 278) propose the new governance model and approach of 'multilevel governance' which means that the 'central state does not monopolise action, but interacts in many different ways with actors at subnational, supranational and international levels'.

Hooghe and Marks (2003: 235) observe that 'governance diffusion and desperation allows for the internalisation of externalities, gives space for heterogeneity and preferences, and allows for multiple arenas of innovation and experimentation'. Our book will provide solid empirical analyses which assess and compare the direct effects from different social actors that form the emerging multilevel governance for renewable energy production, consumption and related social innovation in China and Japan. These entail the comparison of the influence from governmental, business, industrial, legal and research agencies on the adaption, diffusion and sectorally motivated integration of clean energy related SDGs in China and Japan.

Our study tested the underlying hypothesis that, in the transmission and adaptation of global SDGs in different national contexts, three large groups of social actors encompassing sources of information, mediating actors and socio-industrial end-users form, shape and contribute to the complex, latent networks of social engagement. It does so in order to illuminate how the distribution within these networks largely determines the level and breadth of the diffusion of global SDGs and their associated environmentalist norms, knowledge of which is essential for informing policy-making at national and international levels.

As discussed at the outset of this study, there are signs of a rapid transition to a clean/renewable energy system in both China and Japan which indicate sweeping society-level changes in order to fully implement. It will impact significantly on the social, economic and political landscape of East Asia. Further, this transition is influenced by the new metrics and indices championed by the UN as an instrumental institution of global governance which aims to diffuse environmentalist norms globally to accelerate the response to climate change in order to meet the targets set at the Paris Agreement, given its urgency. Despite this, there is very limited research, especially from an empirical perspective, on how this is 'translated' – in other words, how national polities promote new behaviour, practices and visions to encourage a rapid national adaption and diffusion of largely localized versions of the UN SDGs. The current study has made a first effort at probing into the complex social phenomenon of the transmission and cross-cultural translation of SDGs, with a particular focus on people's lifestyle and behavioural change amid the growing political discourse surrounding environmental issues and responsibility, such as conscious consumption of green or renewable energies in China and Japan.

Our study proposed and tested three important social mechanisms which underscore the translation, adaptation and diffusion of discourses on transitioning to clean/renewable energy in the two countries, which represent two distinct social and cultural systems. The three interlinking social mechanisms reveal from different angles the important yet largely under-explored interaction among different social agencies and sectors in the development and diffusion of clean/renewable energy discourses. Specifically, the conceptualization of the proposed social diffusion model entailed the empirical corpus-driven analysis of the strengths of association among three large groups of social agencies and actors. First are the categories of information sources which produce and disseminate localized versions of clean/renewable energy discourse, e.g. top industrial, business and government/political sources. Second are socio-industrial sectors which are actively engaged in the growing clean/renewable energy discourses as part of transitioning to 'low carbon' or 'green' business practices. Third are the media such as newspapers, magazines/journals which operate as intermediary institutions between information sources and the socio-industrial end-users, exerting their own influence by either enhancing or stymying diffusion in certain areas.

Chapter 8 provides corpus-based discourse analyses of the main social factors which contribute to the introduction and cultural adaptation of values, principles and idea sets of environmental sustainability in China. Using a combination of qualitative and quantitative methods to explore large original Chinese multi-sectoral publication databases, this study illustrated the changing patterns and mechanisms underlying the social dissemination and adaptation of sustainability materials in China, providing first-hand evidence of the country's sustainable development strategies and agendas. In terms of methodological innovation, this is the first study which effectively integrates qualitative and quantitative research methodologies from translation studies, Chinese media and discourse analysis and quantitative social sciences. It offers valuable insights into the different stages of the production and development of sustainability translation resources, and the social dissemination and the subsequent utilization of translated sustainable values, concepts and principles in China over the last two decades. The empirical corpus analytical models constructed illustrate the social mechanisms, for example, the proposed multi-sectoral interaction around the social diffusion of translated sustainability materials; and the intra-sectoral framing of the industrial materialization of sustainability goals and principles. These innovative models are first introduced to Chinese environmental translation studies; and can be effectively adapted for the study of the translation and social communication of sustainability in other social and cultural systems, as we witness global trends of transitioning towards sustainable societies and communities. As with many empirical studies, while this study has identified and developed approaches to address some key research questions related to the social diffusion of sustainability translation resources in China, it has also raised new questions that remain to be answered in future research, for example, whether the features, patterns and mechanisms of the social translation, dissemination and industrial materialization of sustainability aims, goals and principles are unique and exclusive to the Chinese society and cultural system. In other words, mechanisms such as multi-sectoral interaction and sectorally motivated framing of the industrial materialization of sustainability principles can also be observed in other countries and/or regions. If this hypothesis holds true, it will provide a strong theoretical basis for the development of analytical methods and procedures to compare different countries and communities regarding their transition towards sustainable societies with distinct local features and characteristics, as a result of the locally based and culturally rooted interpretation and translation of sustainability.

Chapter 9 of the book uses advanced statistics to exploit the large amounts of data available from original, creditable Chinese and Japanese sources. The corpus study developed empirical matrices to measure the varying impact from the main information sources on socio-industrial end-users in terms of the social visibility and engagement level of the latter in the growing clean/renewable energy discourses in East Asia. Corpus analyses point to different direct effects from Chinese and Japanese government/political sources on the visibility of industrial sectors. A number of asymmetrical patterns were identified between the two countries which suggest very different governmental and political focuses and approaches to the promotion of the lifestyle/behavioural change dimension of the clean/renewable energy discourse among industrial sectors. For example, while the Chinese government has actively engaged a number of industrial sectors in the promotion of practices amenable to transitioning to clean/renewable energy among the public such as Agriculture; Alternative Fuels; Business and Consumer Services; Consumer Goods; Electric Power Generation; Leisure and Hospitality; Industrial Goods; Media and Entertainment; Real Estate and Construction; Retail Wholesale; Transport and Logistics; and Utilities; the Japanese government has a strong focus on the Nuclear Fuel; Healthcare and Life Science; and Automotive sectors.

We have also been able to gauge the mediating effects from the mass media, defined as Magazines/Journal and Newspapers, on the dynamic relationships between the information sources and industrial sectors. The results highlight how the mass media can serve as a useful social intervention instrument to influence the development of complex pathways for the diffusion of the clean/renewable energy discourses. The empirical findings from the corpus analysis align with existing knowledge of the distinct role of the media in China and Japan as two contrastive social and cultural systems. For example, our analysis found a strong correlation between Chinese top industry sources and the Chinese media in the discussion of people's lifestyle and behavioural change with the rise of the green and renewable energy consumption. The statistically significant alignment between Chinese top industry sources and Chinese media indicates the lack of independence of the Chinese media from Chinese top industry sources. In contrast, the reporting of the Chinese media on lifestyle/social change vis-à-vis transitioning to a clean/renewable energy system is significantly different from publications on similar issues by government/political sources.

Similarly, the Chinese media takes a different approach from Chinese business sources in communicating this. The corpus analysis shows that the Japanese media have maintained their independence from top industry and government/political sources, and have exhibited a markedly different approach from business sources. This can be explained by the fact that, as confirmed in the corpus analysis, whereas the Japanese business sources have focused more on industrial sectors such as Alternative Fuels; Financial Services; Industrial Goods; Retail and Wholesale; Technology; and Utilities, the Japanese mass media have given more visibility to industrial sectors such as Telecommunication; Electric Power Generation; Consumer Goods; Automotive; and Retail and Wholesale. In addition, another important relationship examined in this study is the MSI among the three large sources of information, i.e. top industry, government/political, business sources and the mass media. The corpus analysis reveals how strong MSI may well serve as an indicator of the efficiency and effectiveness of the social diffusion and communication of the renewable energy discourse. The comparison between the averaged MSI scores computed for China and Japan with their overall country EPI scores displays important consistency. It is argued that the relatively low MSI score (16.386) in China, compared with Japan (22.537) may be an explanatory factor as to why China ranks lower on the widely endorsed EPI.

Overall, the cross-cultural translation, adaptation and dissemination of global SDGs represent a complex social and research issue which has important contemporary significance. It has made a useful and original contribution to the study of global sustainability discourse by illustrating important social mechanisms which underscore the ongoing transition to clean/renewable energy systems in China and Japan in terms of decarbonization, 'low-carbonization' and drastically improving energy efficiency in social infrastructures and day-to-day life. This interdisciplinary and innovative research approach has developed a new line of empirical research for international environmental studies and is applicable to a wide range of social scientific disciplines. Further, the analytical framework developed is data-intensive and largely replicable and can thus be used not only for the study of East Asia, but for the comparative area studies in general. Some of the empirical findings uncovered in our study align with existing knowledge of the different social and cultural systems of China and Japan, for example, in terms of the mediating role of the media and the level of MSI around main information sources. By contrast, some corpus findings have significantly advanced current understanding of the communication of environmental protection and the promotion of renewable energy including the engagement of socio-industrial sectors in the sustainability discourse by information sources in different national contexts. The rest of the book will continue to analyse the diverse dimensions of the growing sustainability discourse in China and Japan, with a view to establishing and contrasting the distinct social transformation models in the region as part of the global transition to renewable energy to meet the levels required to mount an effective response to climate change and the local, national and global level.

Appendix 1

Table A1.1 Mandarin Chinese word list

Chinese term	English translation	Frequency
节能减排	Energy conservation	18,090
环境保护	Environmental protection	15,324
节能环保	Energy saving and environmental protection	11,440
生态文明	Eco-civilization	6792
低碳经济	Low-carbon economy	3850
社会责任	A sense of social responsibility	3754
低能耗	Low energy consumption	3413
环境友好型	Environmentally friendly	3315
绿色经济	Green economy	2404
低碳城市	Low-carbon city	1722
日常生活	Daily life	1506
环保意识	Environmental protection awareness	1481
绿色消费	Green consumption	1412
消费方式	Consumption patterns	1349
技术革命	Technological revolution	1300
步行	Walking	1278
节能低碳	Save energy and exercise low-carbon	1183
绿色出行	Green travel	1174
低碳生活	Low-carbon life	1131
绿色转型	Green transformation	1022
和谐社会	Harmonious society	944
社会责任感	Social responsibility	786
节能宣传	Energy conservation publicity	758
能源消费革命	Energy consumption revolution	674
责任意识	Sense of responsibility	638
绿色生活	Green life	575
低碳理念	Low-carbon concepts	548
环保理念	Environmental protection concept	541
节约用电	Save electricity	517
经营行为	Business behaviour	499
节能意识	Energy awareness	498
低碳节能	Low-carbon and energy-saving principles	488
社会关注	Social concern	477
智能城市	Smart city	460
低碳生活方式	Low-carbon lifestyle	443
安全责任	Safety responsibility	442
行为规范	Behavioural norms	418
社会主义现代化	Socialist modernization	406
自觉行动	Conscious action	372

Appendix 2

Table A2.1 Japanese word list

Japanese term	English translation	Frequency
省エネ	Energy saving	15,013
エコ	Eco	6272
地産地消	Local production	4225
有効活用	Effective utilization of clean energy	3811
環境保全	Environmental protection	3115
低炭素社会	Low carbon society	3068
環境負荷	Environmental load	2884
環境保護	Environmental protection	1724
再生可能エネルギーを活用	Utilize renewable energy	1669
エネルギーマネジメント	Energy management	1550
環境配慮	Environmentally conscious	1496
スマートコミュニティー	Smart community	1289
経済活動	Economic activity	1267
環境に配慮した	Environmentally friendly	1244
循環型社会	Circuity-based society	1211
水素社会	Hydrogen society	1200
持続可能な社会	Sustainable society	1086
スマートコミュニティ	Smart community	1022
見える化	Make visible	1016
環境教育	Environmental education	885
企業活動	Business activities	864
生産活動	Production activities	761
自家消費	Self consumption	750
環境負荷低減	Reduction of environmental impact	738
地域貢献	Regional contribution	698
スマートシティー	Smart city	644
環境意識	Environmental consciousness	609
自給自足	Self-sufficiency	591
国の責任	State responsibility	577
削減義務	Reduction obligation	570
地球環境保全	Global environment conservation	421
消費生活	Consumer life	379
市民生活	Civic life	363
環境活動	Environmental activities	349
省CO2	Saving CO_2	345
産業活動	Industrial activities	333
節電意識	Conservation consciousness	327
環境経営	Environmental management	315
意識改革	Awareness reform	306
国民の負担	Burden of the people	300

References

350.org (n.d.), 'About 350', *350.org*. Available online at https://350.org/about.

Abe, Shinzō (6 October 2013), 'STS fōramu 2013-nen nenji sōkai-ni okeru Abe sōri aisatsu' [Greeting from Prime Minister Abe at the STS Forum 2013 Annual Meeting], *Cabinet Public Relations Office Cabinet Secretariat*. Available online at www.kantei.go.jp/jp/96_abe/statement/2013/1006sts.html.

Abe, Shinzō (17 April 2014), 'Japan samitto 2014 Abe naikaku sōri daijin kichō kōen' [2014 Japan Summit: Keynote speech by Prime Minister Abe], *Cabinet Public Relations Office Cabinet Secretariat*. Available online at www.kantei.go.jp/jp/96_abe/statement/2014/0417kouen.html.

Abe, Shinzō (1 May 2014), 'Shiti shusai kangei bansankai Abe naikaku sōri daijin supīchi' [Welcoming dinner hosted by the City of London: Speech by Prime Minister Abe], *Cabinet Public Relations Office Cabinet Secretariat*. Available online at www.kantei.go.jp/jp/96_abe/statement/2014/0501speech.html.

Abe, Shinzō (20 January 2017), 'Dai hyaku kyū jū san kokkai-ni okeru Abe naikaku sōri daijin shisei hōshin enzetsu' [Prime Minister Abe's policy speech at the 193rd Session of the National Diet], *Cabinet Public Relations Office Cabinet Secretariat*. Available online at www.kantei.go.jp/jp/97_abe/statement2/20170120siseihousin.html.

Anderson, Kevin, and Alice Bows (2011), 'Beyond "dangerous" climate change: Emission scenarios for a new world', *Philosophical Transactions of the Royal Society A: Mathematical, Physical and Engineering Sciences*, 369: 20–44.

Anderson, Kevin, and John Broderick (2017), 'Natural gas and climate change', *Friends of the Earth Europe*. Available online at www.foeeurope.org/NoRoomForGas.

Asayama, Shinichirō (2015), 'Catastrophism toward "opening up" or "closing down"? Going beyond the apocalyptic future and geoengineering', *Current Sociology*, 63(1): 89–93.

Asayama, Shinichirō, and Atushi Ishii (2012), 'Reconstruction of the boundary between climate science and politics: The IPCC in the Japanese mass media, 1988–2007', *Public Understanding of Science*, 23(2): 1–15.

Austen, Ian, and Clifford Krauss (25 January 2017), 'For Justin Trudeau, Canada's leader, revival of Keystone XL upsets a balancing act', *New York Times*. Available online at www.nytimes.com/2017/01/25/world/canada/canada-justin-trudeau-keystone-xl.html.

Banerjee, Neela, Lisa Song and David Hasemyer (16 September 2015), 'Exxon's own research confirmed fossil fuels' role in global warming decades ago', *Inside Climate News*. Available online at https://insideclimatenews.org/content/Exxon-The-Road-Not-Taken.

Beck, Ulrich (2015), 'Emancipatory catastrophism: What does it mean to climate change and risk society?', *Current Sociology*, 63(1): 75–88.

Beck, Ulrich, and Elisabeth Beck-Gernsheim (2002), *Individualization: Institutionalized individualism and its social and political consequences*. London: Sage.

Beck, Ulrich, Anders Blok, David Tyfield, and Joy Yueyue Zhang (2013), 'Cosmopolitan communities of climate risk: Conceptual and empirical suggestions for a new research agenda', *Global Networks*, 13(1): 1–21.

Bennett, W. Lance, and Shanto Iyengar (2008), 'A new era of minimal effects? The changing foundations of political communication', *Journal of Communication*, 58: 707–31.

Bernstein, Steven (2017), 'The United Nations and the governance of sustainable development goals', in N. Kanie and F. Biermann (eds). *Governing through goals: Sustainable development goals as governance innovation*. Cambridge, MA: MIT Press, pp. 213–35.

Bibby, Andrew (5 July 2013), 'Peer-to-peer lending made simply – the co-operative way', *Guardian*. Available online at www.theguardian.com/social-enterprise-network/2013/jul/05/peer-lending-coop-way.

Boelens, Rutgerd (2013), 'Cultural politics and the hydrosocial cycle: Water, power and identity in the Andean highlands', *Geoforum*, 57, 234–47. doi: 10.1016/j.geoforum.2013.02.008.

Bourke, India (12 September 2017), 'CRISPR technologies could help ecosystems cope with climate change', *Genetic Literacy Project*. https://geneticliteracyproject.org/2017/10/12/crispr-technologies-help-ecosystems-cope-climate-change/.

Bradsher, Keith (5 December 2017), 'China will lead an electric car future, Ford's chairman says', *New York Times*. Available online at www.nytimes.com/2017/12/05/business/ford-china- electric-cars.html.

Brulle, Robert J. (2013), 'Institutionalizing delay: Foundation funding and the creation of U.S. climate change counter-movement organization', *Climate Change*. doi: 10.1007/s10584-013-1018-7. Available online at drexel.edu/%7E/media/Files/now/pdfs/Institutionalizing%20Delay%20-%20Climatic%20Change.ashx.

Buckley, Chris (24 October 2017), 'China enshrines "Xi Jinping thought" elevating leader to Mao-like status', *New York Times*. Available online at www.nytimes.com/2017/10/24/world/asia/china-xi-jinping-communist-party.html.

Buckley, Tim, and Simon Nicholas (2017), 'China's global renewable energy expansion: How the world's second-biggest national economy is positioned to lead the world in clean-power investment', *Institute for Energy Economics and Financial Analysis*. Available online at http://ieefa.org/wp-content/uploads/2017/01/Chinas-Global-Renewable-Energy-Expansion_January-2017.pdf.

Burnham, Peter (2001), 'New Labour and the politics of depoliticization', *The British Journal of Politics & International Relations*, 3(2): 127–49.

Carbon Offset Research & Education (2011), 'Radiative forcing', *Stockholm Environment Institute*. Available online at www.co2offsetresearch.org/aviation/RF.html.

Castells, Manuel (2009), *The rise of the network society*. Oxford: Blackwell.

Cavalli-Sforza, L. L., and M. W. Feldman (1980), *Cultural transmission and evolution: A quantitative approach*. Princeton, NJ: Princeton University Press.

Chandler, David L. (22 March 2016), 'New chemistries found for liquid batteries: Grid-scale approach to rechargeable power storage gets new arsenal or possible materials', *MIT News Office*. Available online at http://news.mit.edu/2016/chemistries-liquid-batteries-grid-scale-0322.

Coren, Michael J. (22 October 2017), 'Ladies and gentlemen, the winners and losers of the electric car race (so far)', *WordPress.com VIP*. Available online at https://qz.com/1102552/ladies-and-gentlemen-the-winners-and-losers-of-the-electric-car-race-so-far/.

Deephouse, David L., and Mark Suchman (2008), 'Legitimacy in organizational institutionalism', in Royston Greenwood, Christine Oliver, Kerstin Sahlin and Roy Suddaby (eds). *The SAGE handbook of organizational institutionalism*. London: SAGE Publications Ltd, pp. 49–77.

DeWit, Andrew (2012), 'Japan's energy policy at a crossroads: A renewable energy future?', *Asia-Pacific Journal*, 10, 38(4). Available online at http://apjjf.org/2012/10/38/Andrew-DeWit/3831/article.html.

DeWit, Andrew (2013), 'Japan's rollout of smart cities: What role for the citizens?', *Asia-Pacific Journal*, 11, 24(2). Available online at http://apjjf.org/2014/11/24/Andrew-DeWit/4131/article.html.

DeWit, Andrew (2015), 'Japan's bid to become a world leader in renewable energy', *Asia-Pacific Journal*, 13, 40(2). Available online at http://apjjf.org/-Andrew-DeWit/4385.

DeWit, Andrew (2016), 'Japan's "National Resilience" and the legacy of 3–11', *Asia-Pacific Journal*, 14, 6(1). Available online at http://apjjf.org/2016/06/DeWit.html.

DeWit, Andrew (2017), 'Hioki's smart community and Japan's structural reform', *Asia-Pacific Journal*, 14, 15(10). Available online at http://apjjf.org/2016/15/DeWit.html.

Dezem, Vanessa (19 August 2016), 'Solar sold in Chile at lowest ever, half price of coal', *2017 Bloomberg LP*. Available online at www.bloomberg.com/news/articles/2016-08-19/solar-sells-in-chile-for-cheapest-ever-at-half-the-price-of-coal.

Dobson, Hugo (2017), 'Is Japan really back? The "Abe Doctrine" and global governance', *Journal of Contemporary Asia*, 47(2): 199–224.

Dow Jones (2017), 'Dow Jones Factiva', *Dow Jones*. Available online at www.dowjones.com/products/factiva/.

Drijfhout, Sybren, Sebastian Bathlany, Claudie Beaulieu, Victor Brovkin, Martin Claussen, Chris Huntingford, Marten Scheffer, Giovanni Sgubin and Didier Swingedouw (2015), 'Catalogue of abrupt shifts in Intergovernmental Panel on Climate Change climate models', *PNAS*, E5777–E5786. doi: 10.1073/pnas.1511451112.

Economist, The (9 November 2017), 'Africa might leapfrog straight to cheap renewable electricity and minigrids', *The Economist*. Available online at www. economist.com/news/special-report/21731042-road-ubiquitous-electricity-africa-might-leapfrog-straight-cheap-renewable.

Edney, Kingsley, and Jonathan Symons (2014), 'China and the blunt temptations of geo-engineering: The role of solar radiation management in China's strategic response to climate change', *The Pacific Review*, 27(3): 307–22.

Emerson, J., *et al.* (2010), *Environmental Performance Index*. New Haven, CT: Yale Center for Environmental Law and Policy.

Estrada, Zac (28 September 2017), 'Toyota and Mazda are making a new company to develop electric cars', *Vox media*. www.theverge.com/2017/9/28/16379394/mazda-toyota-new-electric-car-company.

Fawcett, Paul, Matthew Flinders, Colin Hay, and Matthew Wood (2017), *Anti-politics, depoliticization and governance*. Oxford: Oxford University Press.

Ferrer, Eduardo Castello, Jake Rye, Gordon Brander, Tim Savas, Douglas Chambers, Hildreth England and Caleb Harper (2017), 'Personal food computer: A new device for controlled-environment agriculture', *arXiv preprint arXiv:1706.05104*. Available online at https://arxiv.org/abs/1706.05104.

Ford, Liz (19 January 2015), 'Sustainable development goals: All you need to know', *Guardian*. Available online at www.theguardian.com/global-development/2015/jan/19/sustainable-development-goals-united-nations.

Friedman, Lisa (20 August 2015), 'China's fossil fuel pollution has been over-estimated', *Scientific American*. Available online at www.scientificAmerican.com/article/china-s-fossil-fuel-pollution-has-been-overestimated/.

Giddens, Anthony (1991), *Modernity and self-identity: Self and society in the late modern age*. Stanford, CA: Stanford University Press.

Gielen, Dolf, Francisco Boshell and Deger Saygin (2016), 'Climate and energy challenges for materials science', *Nature Materials*, 15: 117–20. doi:10.1038/nmat4545.

Gilek, Michael, Mikael Karlsson, Sebastian Linke and Katarzyna Smolarz (2016), 'Chapter 1 – Environmental governance of the Baltic Sea: Identifying key challenges, research topics and analytical approaches', in Michael Gilek, Mikael Karlsson, Sebastian Linke and Katarzyna Smolarz (eds). *Environmental governance of the Baltic Sea*. MARE Publication Series 10. Springer: Heidelberg, pp. 1–20.

Graves, LeAnne (1 March 2017), 'Abu Dhabi plant to produce region's cheapest electricity from solar', *The National*. Available online at www.thenational.ae/business/abu-dhabi-plant-to-produce-region-s-cheapest-electricity-from-solar-1.29977.

Graves, LeAnne (5 June 2017), 'Dubai set for world's cheapest night-time solar power', *The National*. Available online at www.thenational.ae/business/dubai-set-for-world-s-cheapest-night-time-solar-power-1.35494.

Greenwood, Royston, Christine Oliver, Kerstin Sahlin and Roy Suddaby (eds) (2008), *The SAGE handbook of organizational institutionalism*. London: SAGE Publications Ltd.

Grieves, Wilfrid (13 October 2016), 'Climate change, energy security, and the Arctic under the Obama Presidency', *World Policy Institute*. Available online at https://worldpolicy.org/2016/10/13/climate-change-energy-security-and-the-arctic-under-the-obama-presidency/.

Gupta, Aarti, and Michael Mason (2014), *Transparency in global environmental governance: Critical perspectives*. Cambridge, MA: MIT Press.

Gupta, Joyeeta, and Måns Nilsson (2017), 'Toward a multi-level action framework for sustainable development goals', in Norichika Kanie and Frank Biermann (eds). *Governing through goals: Sustainable development goals as governance innovation*. Cambridge, MA: MIT Press, pp. 275–94.

Haas, Peter (1992), 'Introduction: Epistemic communities and international policy coordination', *International Organization*, 46(1): 1–35.

Hagerstrand, T. (1967), *Innovation diffusion as a spatial process*. Chicago: University of Chicago Press.

Hall, Jessica (8 March 2017), 'New solid-state battery chemistry with glass electrolyte delivers 3 times the capacity', *Ziff Davis LLC*. Available online at www.extremetech.com/extreme/245490-new-solid-state-battery-chemistry-glass-electrolyte-same-guy-pioneered-lithium-ion-cells.

Hamilton, James, and Drew Liming (September 2010), 'Careers in wind energy', *US Department of Labour Statistics*. Available online at www.bls.gov/green/wind_energy/wind_energy.pdf.

Hanley, Steve (18 September 2015), 'Japan pushes forward with hydrogen society ahead of Olympics', *Gas2*, Sustainable Enterprises Media Inc. Available online at http://gas2.org/2015/09/18/japan-pushes-forward-hydrogen-society-ahead-olympics/.

Hatoyama, Yukio (2017), *Datsudainihonshugi: 'seijuku-no jidai'-no kuni-no katachi* [*Escaping the Big Japan Ideology: Forming a nation in an 'era of maturity'*]. Tokyo: Heibonsha.

Hay, Colin (2007), *Why we hate politics*. Malden, MA: Polity Press.

Hook, Glenn D., Julie Gilson, Christopher W. Hughes and Hugo Dobson (2012), *Japan's international relations: Politics, economics and security*. Third edition. Oxon: Routledge.

Hook, Glenn D., Libby Lester, Meng Ji, Kingsley Edney, Chris G. Pope and Luli van der Does-Ishikawa (2017), *Environmental pollution and the media: Political discourses of risk and responsibility in Australia, China and Japan*. Oxon: Routledge.

Hooghe, Liesbeth, and Gary Marks (2003), 'Unraveling the central state, but how? Types of multi-level governance', *American Political Science Review*, 97(2), 233–43.

Hsu, Angel, D. C. Etsy, M. A. Levy, A. de Sherbinin, L. Johnson, O. Malik and M. Jatieh (2016), 'Global metrics for the environment: The Environmental Performance Index ranks countries' performance on high-priority environmental issues', *2016 Environmental Performance Index*. New Haven, CT: Yale University. Available online at https://issuu.com/2016yaleepi/docs/epi2016_final.

Ikeda, Saburo (2013), 'Beyond conventional scope of risk analysis: Lessons from the 3.11 earthquake, tsunami, and Fukushima nuclear disaster', in Saburo Ikeda and Yasunobu Maeda (eds). *Emerging issues learned from the 3.11 disaster as multiple events of earthquake, tsunami and Fukushima nuclear accident*. The

Committee of the Great East Japan Disaster, Society for Risk Analysis, SRA Japan, pp. 15–20. Available online at www.sra-japan.jp/cms/uploads/311Booklet.pdf.

Index Mundi (2017a), 'Crude oil imports by country', *IndexMundi*. Available online at www.indexmundi.com/energy/?product=oil&graph=imports&display=rank.

Index Mundi (2017b), 'Coal imports by country', *IndexMundi*. Available online at www.indexmundi.com/energy/?product=coal&graph=imports&display=rank.

Indigenous Climate Action (2017), 'Building indigenous climate change literacy', *Indigenous Climate Action*. Available online at www.indigenousclimateaction. com/indigenous-climatechangetoolkit.

International Gas Union (2017), '2017 World LNG Report', *IGU*. Available online at www.igu.org/sites/default/files/103419-World_IGU_Report_no%20crops.pdf.

Jacobson, Mark Z. (2017), 'Roadmaps to transition countries to 100% clean, renewable energy for all purposes to curtail global warming, air pollution, and energy risk', *Earth's Future*, 5(10), 948–52.

Jagers, Sverker C., and Johannes Stripple (2003), 'Climate governance beyond the state', *Global Governance*, 9(3): 385–99.

Japan Times (7 March 2015), 'Electricity and gas deregulation', *The Japan Times*. Available online at www.japantimes.co.jp/opinion/2015/03/07/commentary/ japan-commentary/electricity-gas-deregulation/#.WjO_S0uYN98.

Ji, Meng (2018), 'Multi-sectoral interaction in environmental knowledge communication', in Ji Meng and Michael P. Oakes (eds). *Advances in empirical translation studies: Developing data-driven and user-oriented translation resources and technologies for social and knowledge innovation*. Cambridge, UK: Cambridge University Press.

Jinna, Sikina, and Abby Lindsay (2016), 'Diffusion through issue linkage: Environmental norms in US trade agreements', *Global Environmental Politics*, 16(3): 41–61. doi: 10.1162/GLEP_a_00365.

Johnson, Victoria (4 September 2012), 'Unburnable carbon: Rational investment for sustainability', *New Economics Foundation*. Available online at http://new economics.org/2012/09/unburnable-carbon/.

Johnston, Eric (14 October 2017), 'Balance of power: Shift toward renewable energy appears to be picking up steam', *The Japan Times*. Available online at www.japantimes.co.jp/news/2017/10/14/business/balance-power-shift-toward-renewable-energy-appears-picking-steam/#.WjPHuUuYN98.

Joseph, Jonathan (2012), *The social in the global: Social theory, governmentality and global politics*. Cambridge, UK: Cambridge University Press.

Joshi, Devin, and Roni Kay O'Dell (2016), 'The critical role of mass media in international norm diffusion: The case of UNDP Human Development reports', *International Studies Perspective*, 18(3): 343–64. doi: 10.1093/isp/ekv018.

Kanie, Norichika, and Frank Biermann (eds) (2017), *Governing through goals: Sustainable development goals as governance innovation*. Cambridge, MA: MIT Press.

Kankyō Bijinesu Onrain (2012), 'Kankyō yōgo-shū: Shōene-hō (kaisei shōene-hō)' [Environment glossary: Energy Conservation Act (Amended Energy Conservation Act)], *Nippon bijinesu shuppan*. Available online at www.kankyo-business. jp/dictionary/000183.php.

Khullar, Bhavya (4 September 2017), 'Nanomaterials could combat climate change and reduce pollution', *Scientific American*. Available online at www. scientificAmerican.com/article/nanomaterials-could-combat-climate-change-and-reduce-pollution/.

Kingston, Jeff (2013), 'Abe's nuclear energy policy and Japan's future', *Asia-Pacific Journal*, 11, 34(1). Available online at http://apjjf.org/2013/11/34/Jeff-Kingston/3986/article.html.

Klein, Naomi (2013), *This changes everything: Capitalism vs. the climate*. New York: Simon & Schuster.

Klein, Naomi (2017), *No is not enough: Defeating the new shock politics*. UK: Penguin Random House.

Kudō, Aya (2015), 'Chūgoku-no shimbun shihon seisaku-ni miru sinbun tōsei: minkan shihon/gaishi-no sannyū-o meguru shihon seisaku henkō-no bunseki-kara' [Media control and Chinese policy towards the capitalization of newspapers: Analysis of capitalization policy change concerning the introduction of private and foreign capital.], *Waseda seiji kōhō kenkyū*, 108: 19–34.

LaForgia, Rebecca (2017), 'Listening to China's multilateral voice for the first time: Analysing the Asian Infrastructure Investment Bank for soft power opportunities and risks in the narrative of "lean, clean and green"', *Journal of Contemporary China*, 107: 633–49.

Lai, Karyn L. (2008), *An introduction to Chinese philosophy*. Cambridge, UK: Cambridge University Press.

Lenton, Timothy (2013), 'Environmental tipping points', *Annual Review of Environment and Resources*, 38: 1–29.

Lenton, Timothy M. (2014), 'Game theory: Tipping climate cooperation', *Nature Climate Change*, 4(1). doi: 10.1038/nclimate2078.

Leong, Alvin (14 December 2015), 'How the Paris Agreement and the SDGs work together', *17goals.org*. Available online at http://17goals.org/paris-agreement-sdgs/.

Lester, Libby, and Brett Hutchins (2012), 'The power of the unseen: Environmental conflict, the media and invisibility', *Media, Culture & Society*, 34(7): 847–63.

Li, Bengang, Thomas Gasser, Philippe Ciais, Shilong Piao, Shu Tao, Yves Balkanski, Didier Hauglustaine, Juan-Pablo Boisier, Zhuo Chen, Mengtian Huang, Laurent Zhaoxin Li, Yue Li, Hongyan Liu, Junfeng Liu, Shushi Peng, Zehao Shen, Zhenzhong Sun, Rong Wang, Tao Wang, Guodong Yin, Yi Yin, Hui Zeng, Zhenzhong Zheng and Feng Zhou (2016), 'The contribution of China's emissions to global climate forcing', *Nature*, 531: 357–61. doi:10.1038/nature17165.

Linton, Jamie, and Jessica Budds (2014), 'The hydrosocial cycle: Defining and mobilizing a relational-dialectical approach to water', *Geoforum*, 57, 170–80. doi:10.1016/j.geoforum.2013.10.008.

Liu, Zhu, Dabo Guan, Wei Wei, Steven J. Davis, Philippe Ciais, Jin Bais, Shushi Peng, Qiang Zhang, Klaus Hubacek, Gregg Marland, Robert J. Andres, Douglas Crawford-Brown, Jintai Lin, Hongyan Zhao, Chaopeng Hong, Thomas A. Boden, Kuishuang Feng, Glen P. Peters, Fengming Xi, Junguo Liu, Yuan Li, Yu Zhao, Ning Zeng and Kebin He (2015), 'Reduced carbon emission estimates from fossil fuel combustion and cement production in China', *Nature*, 524(7265): 335–8. doi: 10.1038/nature14677.

Locavesting (7 November 2017), 'A new credit union will focus on clean energy', *Locavesting*. Available online at www.locavesting.com/new-economy/a-new-credit-union-will-focus-on-clean- energy/.

Lombrana, Laura Millan (31 March 2017), 'Company that offered cheapest solar sees prices falling more', *Bloomberg*. Available online at www.bloomberg.com/news/articles/2017-12-04/five-things-you-need-to-know-to-start-your-day-jasrjh2g.

Mahajan, V., and R. A. Peterson (1985), *Models for innovation diffusion*. Newbury Park, CA: Sage Publications.

Mann, Geoff, and Joel Wainwright (2018), *Climate Leviathan: A political theory of our planetary future*. London: Verso.

Marshall, George (2014), *Don't even think about it: Why our brains are wired to ignore climate change*. New York: Bloomsbury Publishing Plc.

Mason, Paul (2015), *Postcapitalism: A guide to our future*. London: Penguin Books.

Mathews, John A. (2016), 'The Asian Super Grid', *Asia-Pacific Journal*, 10, 48(1). Available online at http://apjjf.org/-John_A_-Mathews/3858.

Mathews, John A., and Hao Tan (2014), 'China's continuing renewable energy revolution: Global implications', *Asia-Pacific Journal*, 12, 12(3). Available online at http://apjjf.org/2014/12/44/John-A.-Mathews/4209.html.

Mattauch, Melanie (9 May 2016), 'Keep it in the ground! Just how much exactly?', *350.org*. Available online at https://350.org/keep-it-in-the-ground-just-how-much-exactly/.

McAdam, Doug, and Dieter Rucht (1993), 'The cross national diffusion of movement ideas', *The Annals of the American Academy of Political and Social Science*, 1 July.

Ministry of Industry and Information Technology, China (19 May 2015), 'Zhongguo zhizao 2025 jiedu zhi yi: Zhongguo zhizao 2025, woguo zhizao qiangguo jianshe de hongwei lantu' [China Manufacturing 2025 Interpretation: China Manufacturing 2025, the grand blueprint for building a powerful nation], Beijing: Ministry of Industry and Information Technology. Available online at www.miit.gov.cn/n1146295/n1652858/n1653018/c3780656/content.html.

Ministry of Industry and Information Technology, China (16 May 2017), 'Xijinping zhuchi "yidai yilu" guoji hezuo gaofeng luntan yuanzhuo fenghui bing zhici' [Xi Jinping chairs the roundtable summit of the 'Belt and Road' forum for international cooperation and delivers a speech], Beijing: *Ministry of Infrastructure and Information Technology*. Available online at www.miit.gov.cn/n1146290/n1146392/c5644435/content.html.

Ministry of Industry and Information Technology, China (14 November 2017), 'Zhongguo gongye lüse ditan fazhan "huiyi zai di 23 jie lianheguo qihou dahui qijian chenggong juban"' [Meeting on 'China's industrial green low-carbon development' held successfully during the 23rd UN Climate Conference], Beijing: Ministry of Industry and Information Technology of the People's Republic of China. Available online at www.miit.gov.cn/n1146290/n1146402/n1146440/c5905706/content.html.

Morales, Alex, and Stefan Nicola (3 November 2014), 'Fossil fuel caps urged as scientists warn of climate woes', *Bloomberg*.

Morris, Charles (9 April 2017), 'Beyond lithium: Tesla's partner Panasonic hints at electric vehicle battery improvements', *EVANNEX®*. Available online at https://evannex.com/blogs/news/on-beyond-lithium.

Morris, David Z. (10 September 2017), 'China aims to push gas-powered cars out of the market', *Time Inc*. Available online at http://fortune.com/2017/09/10/electric-cars-china/.

Mufson, Steven (17 May 2012), 'U.S. imposes tariffs on Chinese solar panels', *Washington Post*. Available online at www.washingtonpost.com/business/economy/us-imposes-tariffs-on-chinese-solar-panels/2012/05/17/gIQAz59XWU_story.html?utm_term=.c95beb55a3e4.

Nadesan, Majia Holmer (2010), *Governing childhood into the 21st century: Biopolitical technologies of childhood management and education*. New York: Palgrave Macmillan.

Nagasaka, Toshinari (2013), 'The Great East Japan Earthquake and issues of risk governance and risk communication in complex and multiple LPHC type of disasters – and report from the society for risk analysis in Japan', in Saburo Ikeda and Yasunobu Maeda (eds). *Emerging issues learned from the 3.11 disaster as multiple events of earthquake, tsunami and Fukushima nuclear accident*. The Committee of the Great East Japan Disaster, Society for Risk Analysis, SRA Japan, pp. 7–10. Available online at www.sra-japan.jp/cms/uploads/311Booklet.pdf.

New Energy and Industrial Technology Development Organization (1 August 2017), 'Saisei kanō enerugī-ni yoru CO_2 furī suiso-no jisshō shiken-o kaishi' [Verification tests for CO_2-hydrogen based on renewable energy begins], *New Energy and Industrial Technology Development Organization*. Available online at www.nedo.go.jp/news/press/AA5_100810.html.

Oil Change International (2016), 'The sky's limit: Why the Paris climate goals require a managed decline of fossil fuel production', Washington: Oil Change International. Available online at http://priceofoil.org/content/uploads/2016/09/OCI_the_skys_limit_2016_FINAL_2.pdf.

Oreskes, Naomi, and Erik M. Conway (2010), *Merchants of doubt: How a handful of scientists obscured the truth on issues from tobacco smoke to global warming*. New York: Bloomsbury Press.

People's Climate Movement (n.d.), '2018 Platform: Climate, jobs and justice', *peoplesclimate.org*. Available online at https://peoplesclimate.org/wp-content/uploads/2017/11/pcm.demands.2018.pdf.

Phillips, Tom (19 October 2017), '"A huge deal" for China as the era of Xi Jinping thought begins', *Guardian*. Available online at www.theguardian.com/world/2017/oct/19/huge-deal-china-era-of-xi-jinping-thought-politics.

Pope, Chris G. (13 January 2018), 'China wants to dominate the world's green energy markets – here's why', *The Conversation Media Group*. Available online at https://theconversation.com/china-wants-to-dominate-the-worlds-green-energy-markets-heres-why-89708.

Reuters (22 February 2016), 'China to close more than 1,000 coal mines in 2016: Energy bureau', *Reuters*. Available online at www.reuters.com/article/us-china-energy-coal/china-to-close-more-than-1000-coal-mines-in-2016-energy-bureau-idUSKCN0VV0U5.

Rogers, Everett M. (2010), *Diffusion on innovations*. 4th edition. New York: The Free Press.

Schmidt, Vivian (2008), 'Discursive institutionalism: The explanatory power of ideas and discourse', *Annual Review of Political Science*, 11: 303–26. doi: 10.1146/annurev.polsci.11.060606.135342.

Sekizawa, Jun (2013), 'Appropriate risk governance on radionuclide contamination in food in Japan', in Saburo Ikeda and Yasunobu Maeda (eds). *Emerging issues learned from the 3.11 disaster as multiple events of earthquake, tsunami and Fukushima nuclear accident.* The Committee of the Great East Japan Disaster, Society for Risk Analysis, SRA Japan, pp. 31–5. Available online at www.sra-japan.jp/cms/uploads/311Booklet.pdf.

Setouchi, Jakuchō, Kamata Satoshi, Iida Tetsunari, Miyadai Shinji, Itō Seikō, Oguma Eiji, Mōri Yoshitaka, Tsurumi Wataru, Inaba Tsuyoshi, Matsumoto Hajime, Yamamoto Tarō, Amamiya Karin, Karatani Kōjin, Yamashita Hikaru, Futatsugi Shin, Nakamura Runan, Genpatsu iranai Fukushima-no On'na-tachi, Ochiai Keiko, Koide Hiroaki, Hirai Gen, Sakamoto Ryūichi, Tanaka Yūko, Mutō Ruiko and Takahashi Makoto (2012), *Datsu genpatsu-to demo: soshite, minshushugi [De-nuclear and protest: And then, democracy]*. Tokyo: Chikuma Shobō.

Shane, Daniel (20 September 2017), 'China is winning electric cars "arms race"', *Cable News Network*. Available online at http://money.cnn.com/2017/11/20/investing/lithium-china-electric-car-batteries/index.html.

Shapiro, Judith (2001), *Mao's war against nature: Politics and the environment in revolutionary China*. Cambridge, UK: Cambridge University Press.

Slezak, Michael (6 January 2017), 'China cementing global dominance of renewable energy and technology', *Guardian*. Available online at www.theguardian.com/environment/2017/jan/06/china-cementing-global-dominance-of-renewable-energy-and-technology.

Spracklen, Dominick V. (2016), 'Global warming: China's contribution to climate change', *Nature*, 531: 310–12. doi: 10.1038/531310a.

Stacey, Kiran (16 May 2016), 'From the pitch to the boardroom: International footballer Mathieu Flamini kept his biotech company secret from family and teammates', *The Financial Times*. Available online at www.ft.com/content/9ce7490c-184e-11e6-bb7d-ee563a5a1cc1.

Statoil (21 January 2015), 'Why the world isn't ready for renewable energy – and how we can be', *Forbes Media*. Available online at www.forbes.com/sites/statoil/2015/01/12/how-4d-modelling-is-transforming-energy-exploration-2/#1b2b615c3a7b.

Stockwin, Arthur, and Kweku Ampiah (2017), *Rethinking Japan: The politics of contested nationalism*. Maryland: Lexington Books.

Stoker, Gerry (2002), 'Governance as theory: Five propositions', *International Social Science Journal*, 50(155): 17–28.

Strang, David, and John W. Meyer (1993), 'Institutional conditions for diffusion', *Theory and Society*, 22: 487–511.

Suchman, Mark C. (1995), 'Managing legitimacy: Strategic and institutional approaches', *Academy of Management Review*, 20(3): 571–610.

Szerszynski, Bronislaw, Matthew Kearnes, Phil Macnaghten, Richard Owen and Jack Stilgoe (2013), 'Why solar radiation management geoengineering and democracy won't mix', *Environment and Planning A*, 45: 2809–16.

Thompson, John B. (2005), 'The new visibility', *Theory, Culture & Society*, 22: 31–51. doi: 10.1177/0263276405059413.

Thompson, Lonnie G. (2010), 'Climate change: The evidence and our options', *The Behavior Analyst*, 33(2): 153–70.

Tracy, Elena F., Evgeny Shvarts, Eugene Simonov and Mikhail Babenko (2017), 'China's new Eurasian ambitions: The environmental risks of the Silk Road Economic Belt', *Eurasian Geography and Economics*, 58(1): 56–88. Available online at http://dx.doi.org/10.1080/15387216.2017.1295876.

UNFCCC (2018), 'The Paris Agreement', 2018 United Nations Framework Convention on Climate Change. Available online at https://unfccc.int/process-and-meetings/the-paris-agreement/the-paris-agreement.

van der Does-Ishikawa, Luli, and Glenn D. Hook (2017), 'Mediating risk communication and the shifting locus of responsibility', in Glenn D. Hook, Libby Lester, Meng Ji, Kingsley Edney, Chris G. Pope, and Luli van der Does-Ishikawa (eds). *Environmental pollution and the media: Political discourses of risk and responsibility in Australia, China and Japan*. Oxon: Routledge.

Vaughn, Adam (5 July 2017), 'All Volvo cars to be electric or hybrid from 2019', *Guardian*. Available online at www.theguardian.com/business/2017/jul/05/volvo-cars-electric-hybrid-2019.

Wakuta, Yukihiro (2015), 'Ajenda settingu-ni okeru imi nettowāku-to furēmingu: "chisan chishō-o jirei-to shite"' [The meaning network and framing in agenda setting: A case study on 'local production for local consumption'], *Nihon Jōhō Keiei Gakkaishi*, 35(3): 4–7.

Wakuta, Yukihiro (2016), 'Seidoka-no furēmuwāku kōchiku-no shiron' [Constructing a framework for institutionalization], *Shōgaku ronsan (Chūō Daigaku)*, 57(5–6): 337–61.

Wattles, Jackie (3 June 2017), 'India to sell only electric cars by 2030', *Cable News Network*. Available online at http://money.cnn.com/2017/06/03/technology/future/india-electric-cars/index.html.

Weber, Max (1978), *Economy and society: An outline of interpretive sociology*. Berkeley, CA: University of California Press.

West, Cornell (2005), *Democracy matters: Winning the fight against imperialism*. New York: Penguin Group.

Williamson, Piers (2014), 'Demystifying the official discourse on childhood thyroid cancer in Fukushima', *Asia-Pacific Journal*, 12, 49(2). Available online at http://apjjf.org/2014/12/49/Piers-Williamson/4232.html.

Wood, Matt, and Matthew Flinders (2014), 'Rethinking depoliticisation: Beyond the governmental', *Policy & Politics*, 42(2): 151–70.

WWF (2016), 'Living Planet Report 2016: Risk and resilience in a new era', Gland, Switzerland: WWF International. Available online at http://awsassets.panda.org/downloads/lpr_living_planet_report_2016.pdf.

Xinhua News Agency (7 September 2015), 'Guojia nengyuan ju juzhang Nu Er-Baikeli jiedu "pei dian wang jianshe gaizao xingdong jihua (2015–2020) nian"' [An interpretation of National Energy Administration secretary, Nur Bekri: 'The distribution network construction and reform action plan (2015–2020)'], *Zhongguo zhengfu wang*. Available online at www.gov.cn/zhengce/2015-09/07/content_2926444.htm.

Xinhua News Agency (23 July 2017), 'Lüse nengyuan shidai-de Zhongguo dandang', *XINHUA.com*. Available online at www.xinhuanet.com//fortune/2017-07/23/c_1121365856.htm.

Xinhua News Agency (27 October 2017), 'Xi Jinping zai zhongguo gongchandang di shijiu ci quanguo daibiao dahui shang de baogao' [Xi Jinping's speech at the Chinese Communist Party's 19th National Congress], *Zhongguo Hulianwang Xinwen Zhongxin*. Available online at www.china.com.cn/19da/2017-10/27/content_41805113.htm.

Xu, Yangyang, and Veerabhadran Ramanathan (2016), 'Well below 2°C: Mitigation strategies for avoiding dangerous to catastrophic climate changes', *PNAS*, 114(39): 10315–23. doi: 10.1073/pnas.1618481114.

Young, Oran R. (2017), *Governing complex systems: Social capital for the Anthropocene*. Cambridge, MA: MIT Press.

Yu, Haichun (2017), 'Chūgoku-no jōhō kanri taisei-ni okeru onrain nyūsu-no jōhōgen-no shūchū' [Concentration of online news information sources and the Chinese information management system], *Masu comyunikēshon kenkyū*, 90: 83–104. Available online at https://doi.org/10.24460/mscom.90.0_83.

Yuasa, Harumichi (2012), 'Sumāto mētā-no hō-teki kadai' [Legal issues to do with smart meters], Kyushu International University, Departmental Bulletin Paper. Available online at https://ci.nii.ac.jp/els/contentscinii_20171215221935.pdf?id=ART0009921495.

Zhang, Lihong (2017), 'Legal framework and practice for environmental protection and application of green energy in China', *International Journal of Ambient Energy*, 38: 489–96.

Index

Printed in the United States
by Baker & Taylor Publisher Services